I0793469

AFTER

AFTER

The Silence of the Lower 9th Ward

JOHN ROSENTHAL

PREFACE BY LOLIS ERIC ELIE

AFTERWORD BY JOHN POPE

SAFE HARBOR BOOKS

ISBN: 978-0-9798226-7-4

LIBRARY OF CONGRESS CONTROL NUMBER: 2014944058

PRINTED AND BOUND IN CHINA

SAFE HARBOR BOOKS
31 PAGE AVENUE
ASHEVILLE, NC 28801

To my dear Paula—always there

FOREWORD

By the time John Rosenthal got to post-flood New Orleans in 2007, the rooftops were no longer populated, the evacuees had evacuated and the President had come and gone. The spectacle had dissipated and with it, you might think, had the chance for spectacular photographs.

"By the time I got there it was a very quiet place," he recalls. "The only photographers I encountered were in tour buses."

So much had been written and shouted about the plight of the Lower 9th Ward that it was more of a cause than a place. The liberals saw it as exhibit A in their case against "small government." The conservatives saw it as a model for the remaking of urban America. Rosenthal didn't see it in such crass political terms.

"When I first saw the Lower 9th Ward I knew instantly that the media had missed the point. It was, simply, a stricken neighborhood, sitting there in a deep and tragic silence."

These photographs, first exhibited at the New Orleans African American Museum in 2008, are pictures of a community. Spectacular pictures in their way. There are churches and front yards and signs and stores. Everything you need for a community is here, save people. The power of these photographs is that you feel the human presence and its absence in every frame of Rosenthal's work.

In those confusing days of 2007, when it seemed that all of the help and most of the hope had come and gone, the most striking feature of New Orleans' most devastated neighborhoods was how much humanity had been left amid the debris. It is this humanity that John Rosenthal captured with a sensitive eye and masterful technique.

Things are better now. People have moved back to New Orleans, though the 9th Ward still lags behind the rest of the city in repopulation. But even if that neighborhood achieves unprecedented levels of population and prosperity, John Rosenthal's work will endure as a portrait, not only of the Lower 9th Ward, but of the strange and haunting beauty made possible by the most terrible of circumstances.

LOLIS ERIC ELIE

PREFACE

Photographing the Lower 9th

I drove into the 9th Ward a year and a half after Katrina left it in ruins. Friends of mine who had already been there told me the devastation was "unbelievable." I wondered what that meant—unbelievable.

My friends were wrong.

The 9th Ward, in its ruin, was believable, but only in the way certain dreams are believable. Post-World War III dreams. Miles and miles of empty houses. No voices, no cars—an eerie silence except for the distant rumble of dump trucks, the occasional crunching of wood. Now and then a darkened limo would drive through. The initial documentary Gold Rush—photography inspired by overturned houses, cars in trees, and mountains of debris—was plainly over. Dramatic spectacle had given way to pervasive loss—a condition far less tangible and difficult to photograph. I'm not sure what I felt about what I saw. Disbelief? To be honest, I wasn't able to grasp the disaster. It was too large to be emotionally comprehended, especially by someone who didn't live there.

Then, despite my original intentions not to, I began to take photographs—photographs that reminded me not so much of the New York photographs I took in the early 1970s, but of the fundamental reasons why I even became a photographer. In those early years I'd walk around the city for days (as

I imagined Cartier-Bresson had walked around Paris) searching for something to photograph—a person, a dog, a store window, a movie marquee, anything that might open up and reveal an idea about life in New York City. One afternoon, however, as I watched a wrecking ball punch holes in a building I had admired only the week before, the thought crossed my mind that whole sections of the city—particularly the parts with a distinct cultural identity—were beginning to disappear. This image of the disappearing city stayed with me, and, almost immediately, I began to photograph everything I considered imperiled—seltzer bottles stacked high in old wooden crates, Ukrainian men playing backgammon in Tompkins Square, a three-masted model of a ship in the dusty window of an Italian seamen's club in Little Italy. I'm glad I took those photographs. The parts of the city I intended to fix in memory have largely disappeared. And since that time, for more than 30 years, using photography as a means to memorialize loss has served as the wellspring of my work.

By the time I arrived in the 9th Ward in the winter of 2007, a large part of the neighborhood had already disappeared, and the rest was in danger of being hauled away. Those who'd lived in the Lower 9th—and who might have considered these silent homes as a proper subject to document—were gone, scraping by in places like Shreveport and Houston.

During that year the only cameras I ever saw belonged to tourists in tour buses.

I wanted the photographs to say "This was here, and that was there." For a photographer, that seemed to be a simple and legitimate task. After all, the moment we forget the intimate details of a Somewhere, it may turn into a glistening Nowhere—monolithic, impersonal, luxurious, and white. The Lower 9th was disappearing, it seemed to me, not only because of Katrina, but because of a long-standing indifference to the poor, an indifference now transforming itself into a mercilessly strategic land-grab.

Photographs, though, not only remember, they register surprise. And what surprised me most about the 9th Ward were the leftover particulars of a multi-layered human geography. What did I expect to find there? The media invariably headline poverty and crime, but those words, chanted like a mantra, don't reveal or illuminate anything; they merely divert us from the deeper problem of American racism. In fact, what I found and what I photographed, weren't the remnants of a dangerous and dilapidated neighborhood now demolished by a hurricane, but the vestiges of a working-class community in which aspiration contended with scarcity, and where religious faith found expression on every block. From my perspective, the floodwaters had washed away not only bricks and mortar, but also the toxic stereotypes that separate us from each other. What was left, in other words, was the vanishing common ground, and it is this familiar terrain that I have photographed.

J.R.

AFTER

1. FULL GOSPEL DELIVERANCE

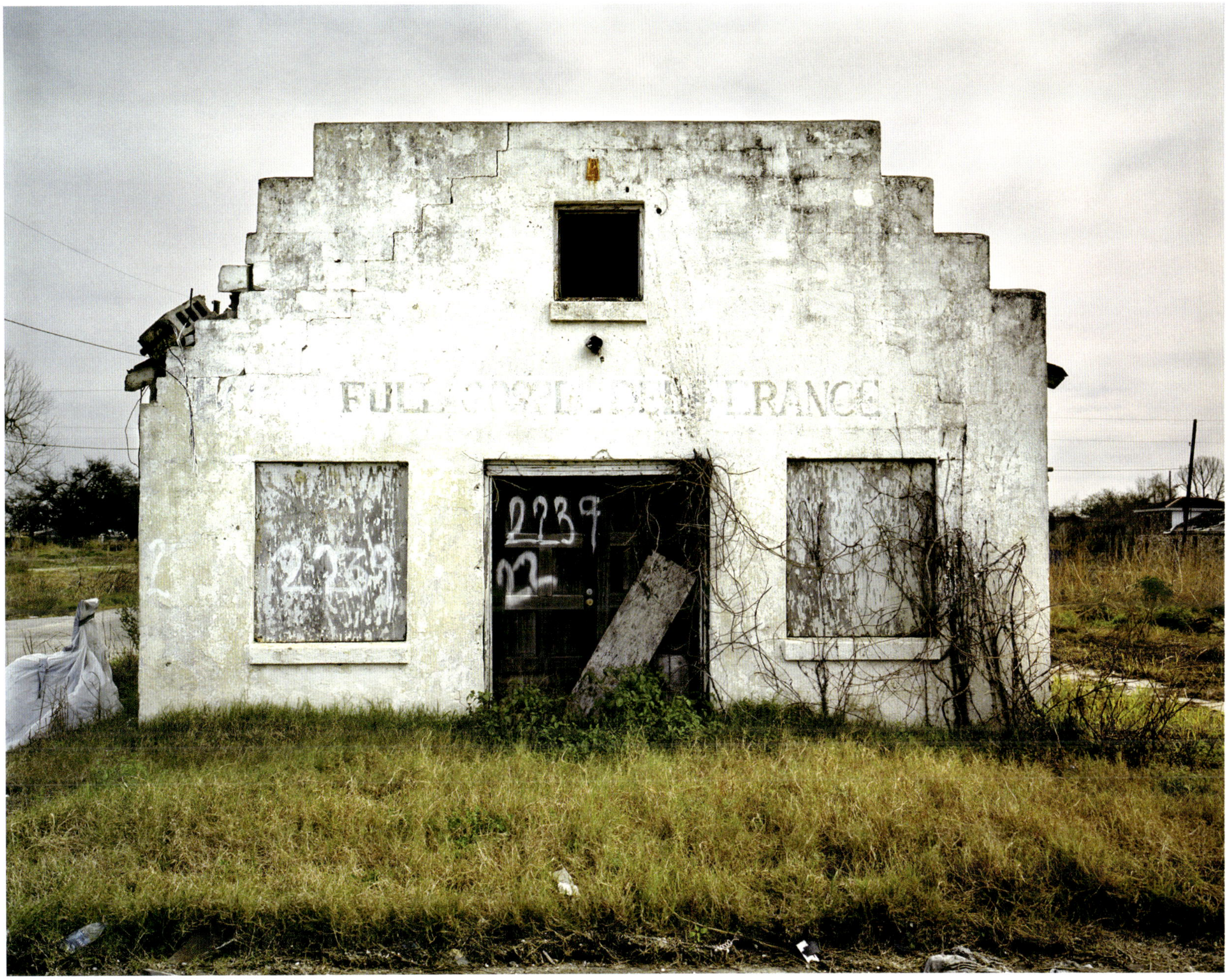
2239

2. ISRAEL UNIVERSAL DIVINE CHURCH

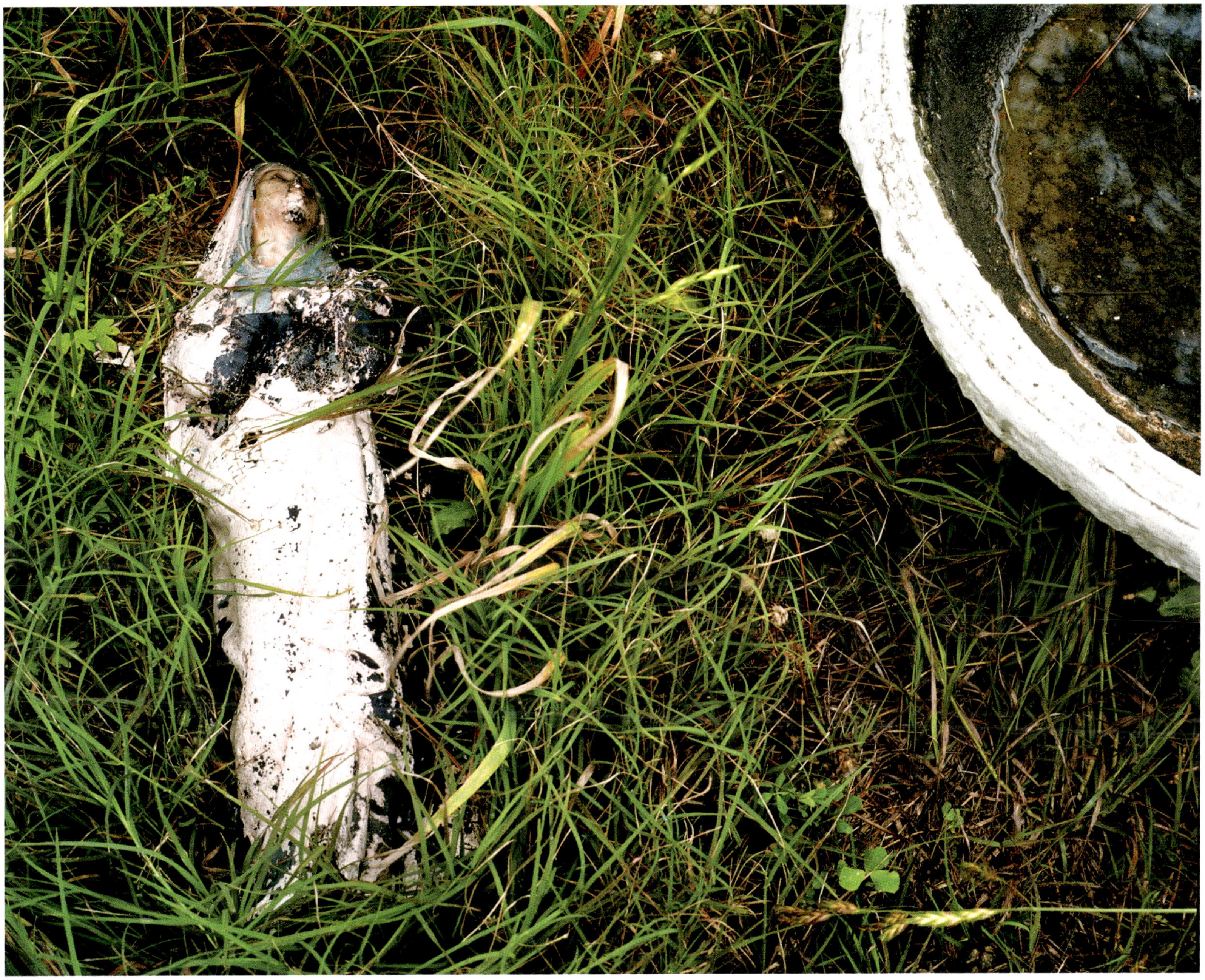

3. HARRIET TUBMAN

LOUIS ARMSTRONG ELEMENTARY SCHOOL

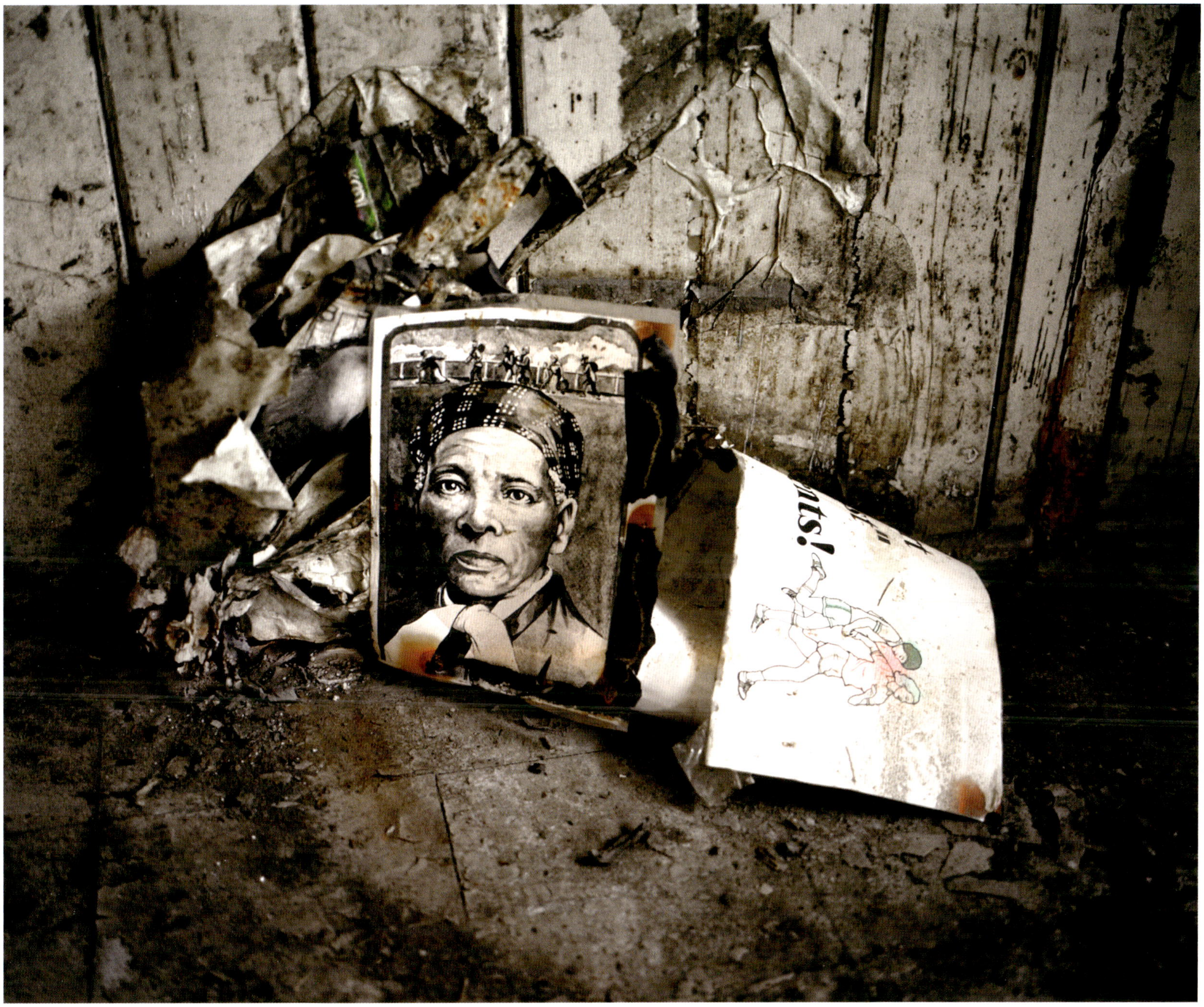

4. WINTHROP STREET

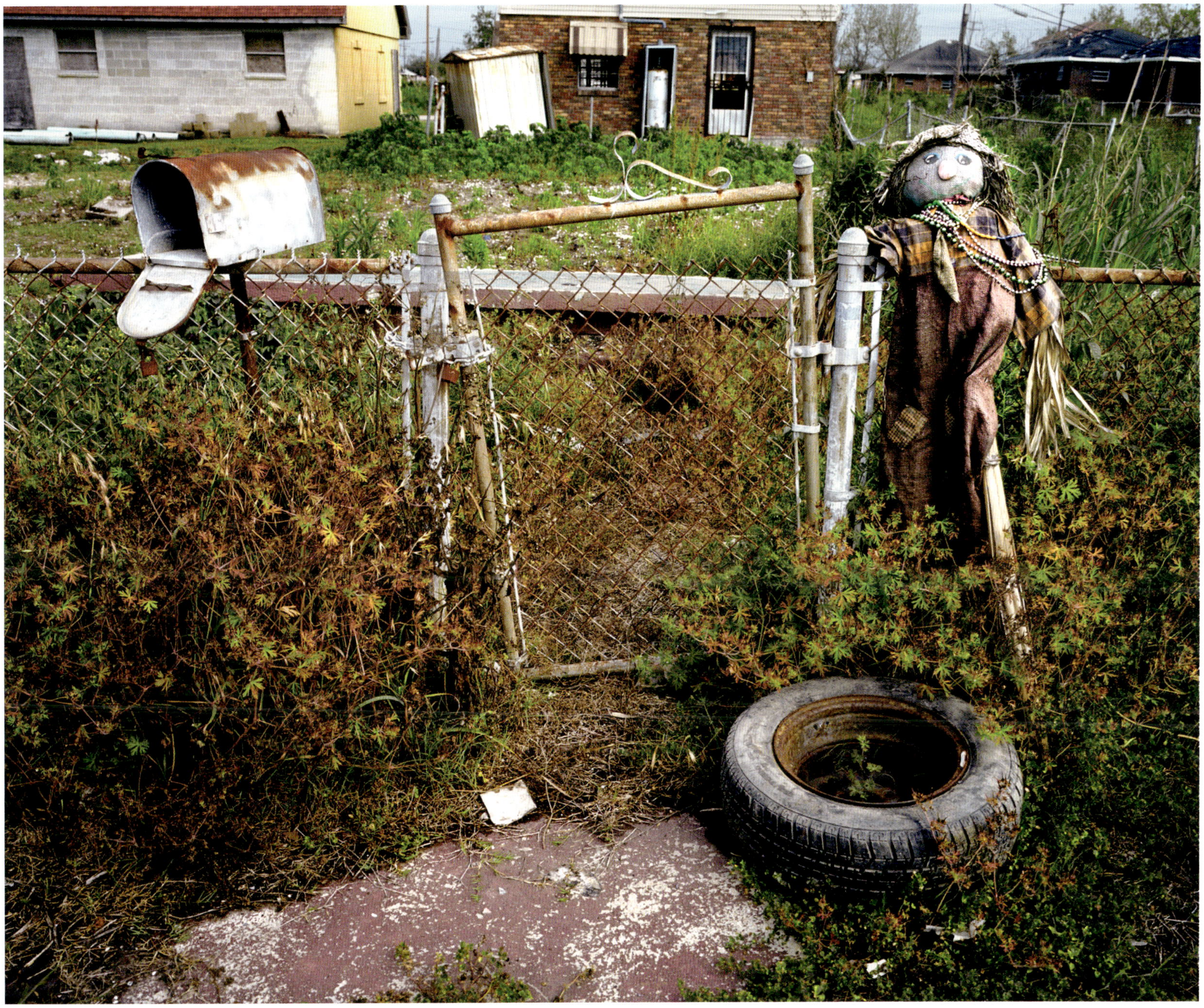

5. FORSTALL STREET

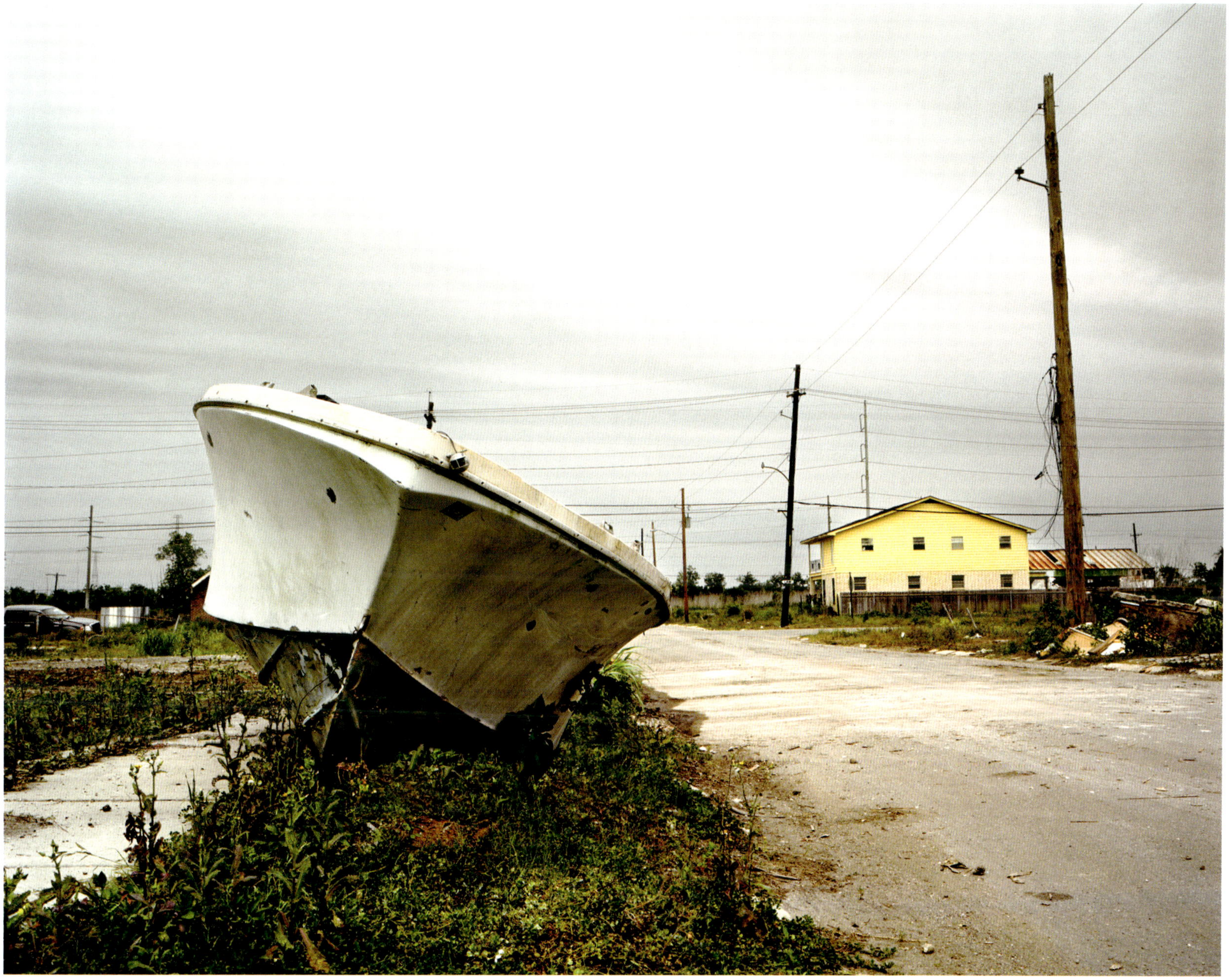

6. RECEPTION HALL

ST. MAURICE AVENUE

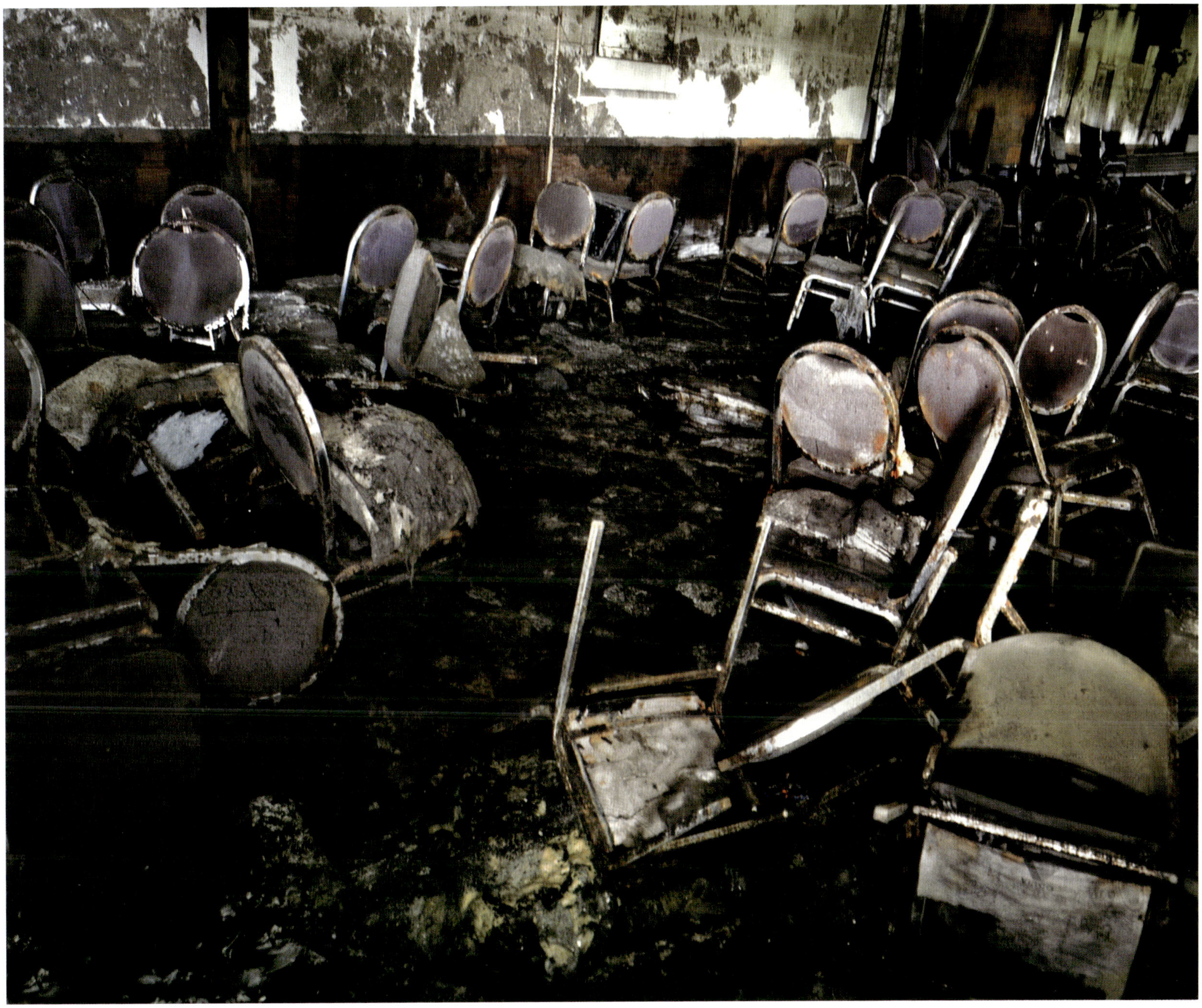

7. SAINT LUKE BAPTIST CHURCH
DORGENOIS STREET

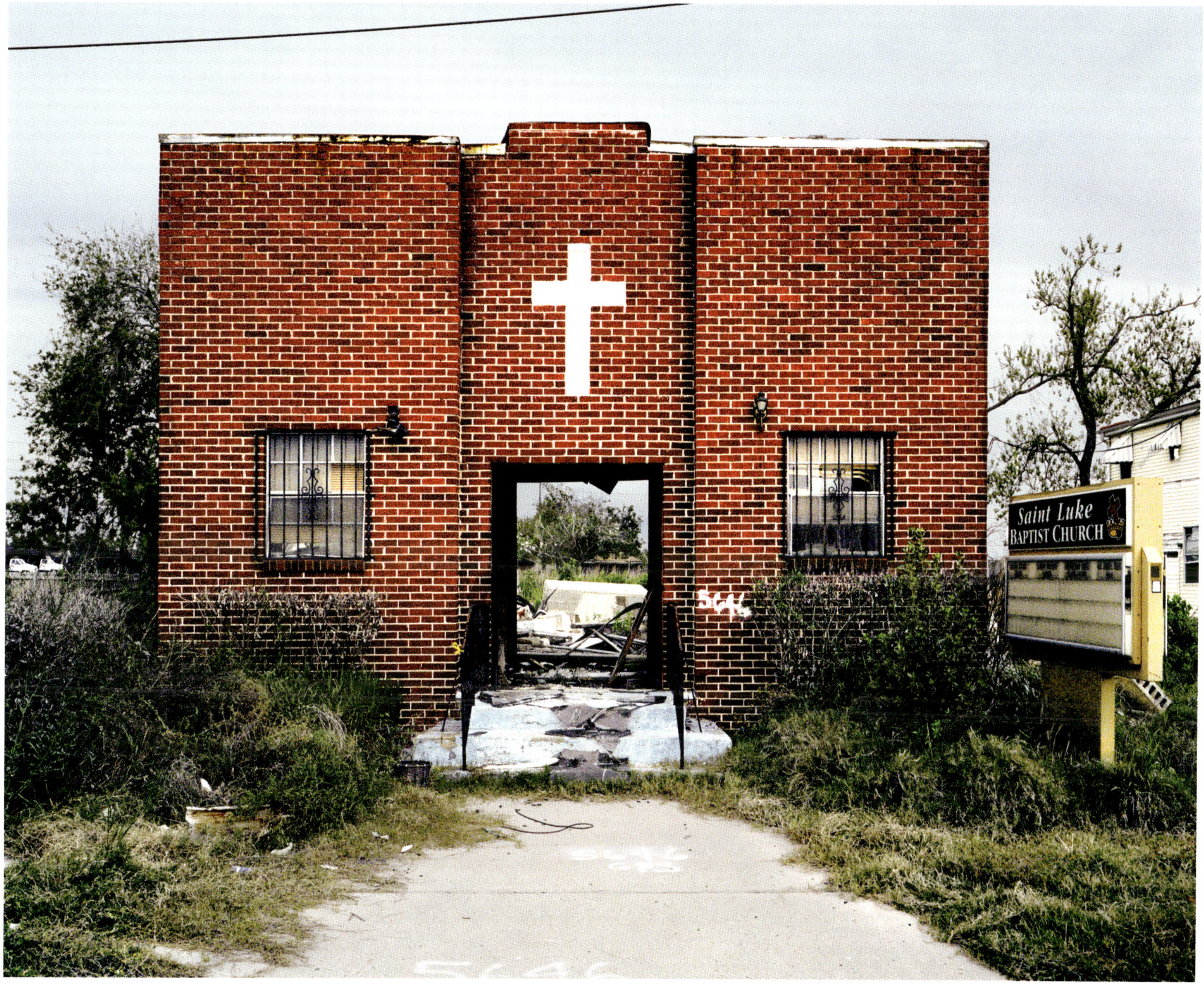
Saint Luke
BAPTIST CHURCH

8. TENNESSEE STREET

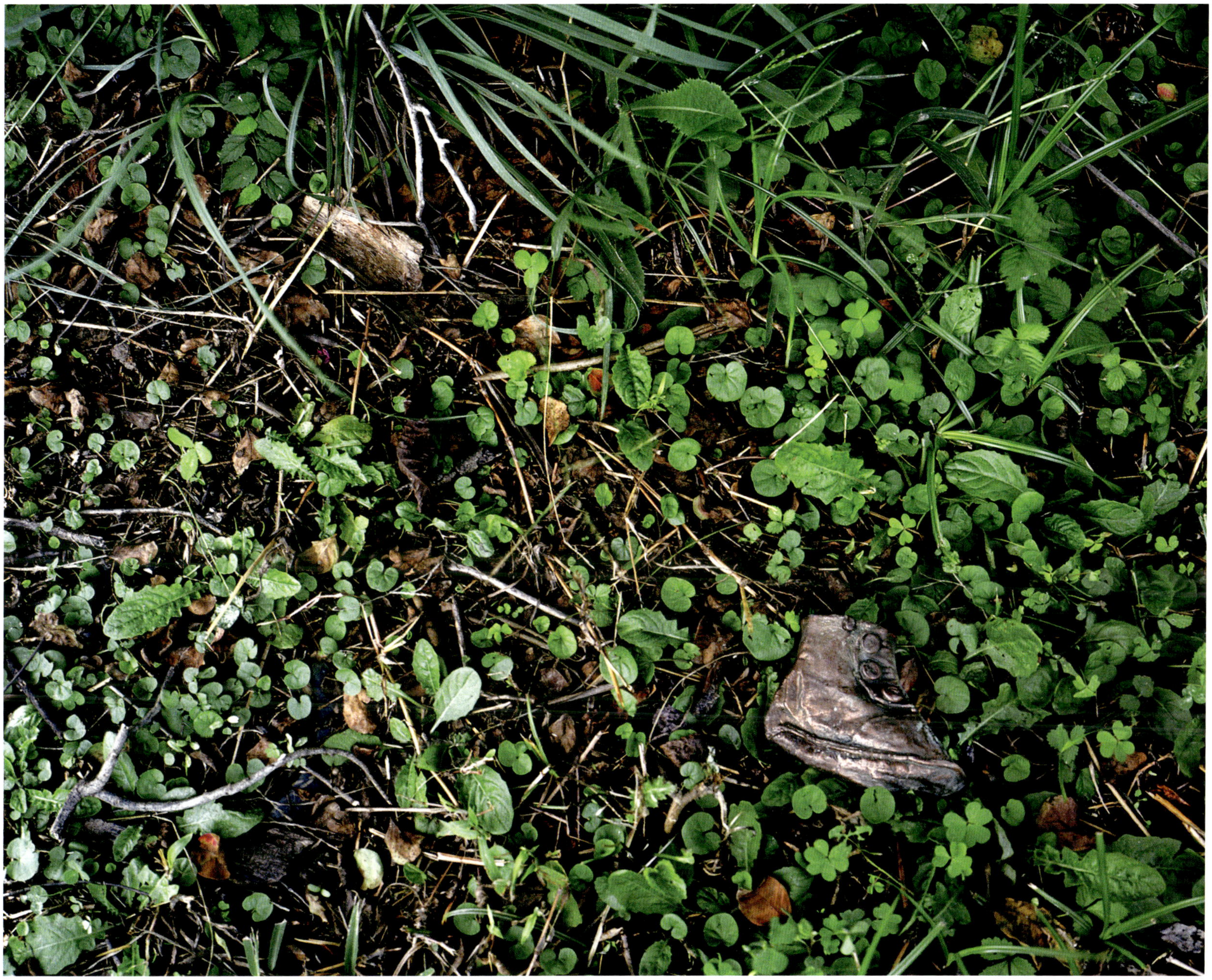

9. ISRAEL UNIVERSAL DIVINE CHURCH

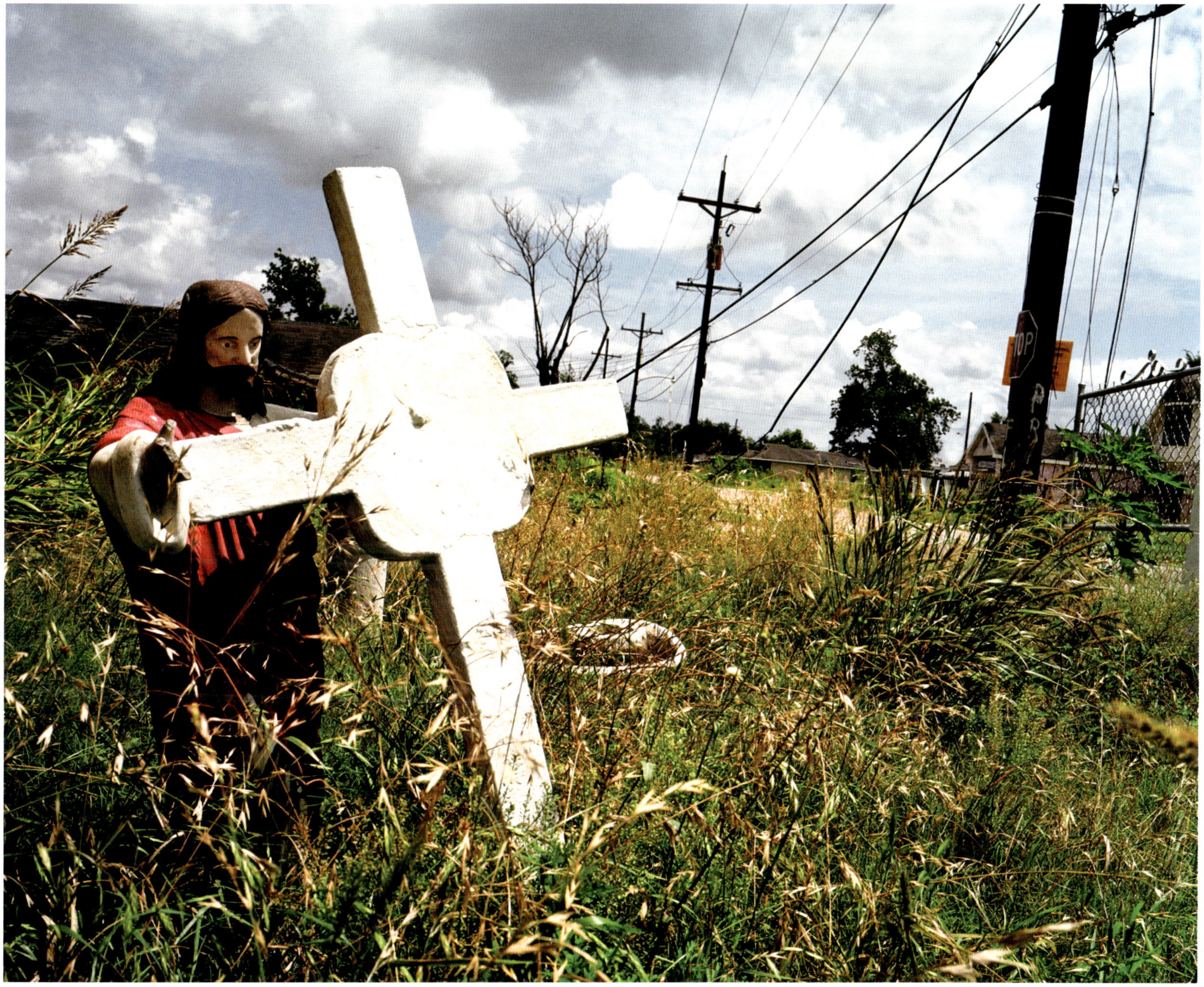

10. DERBIGNY STREET

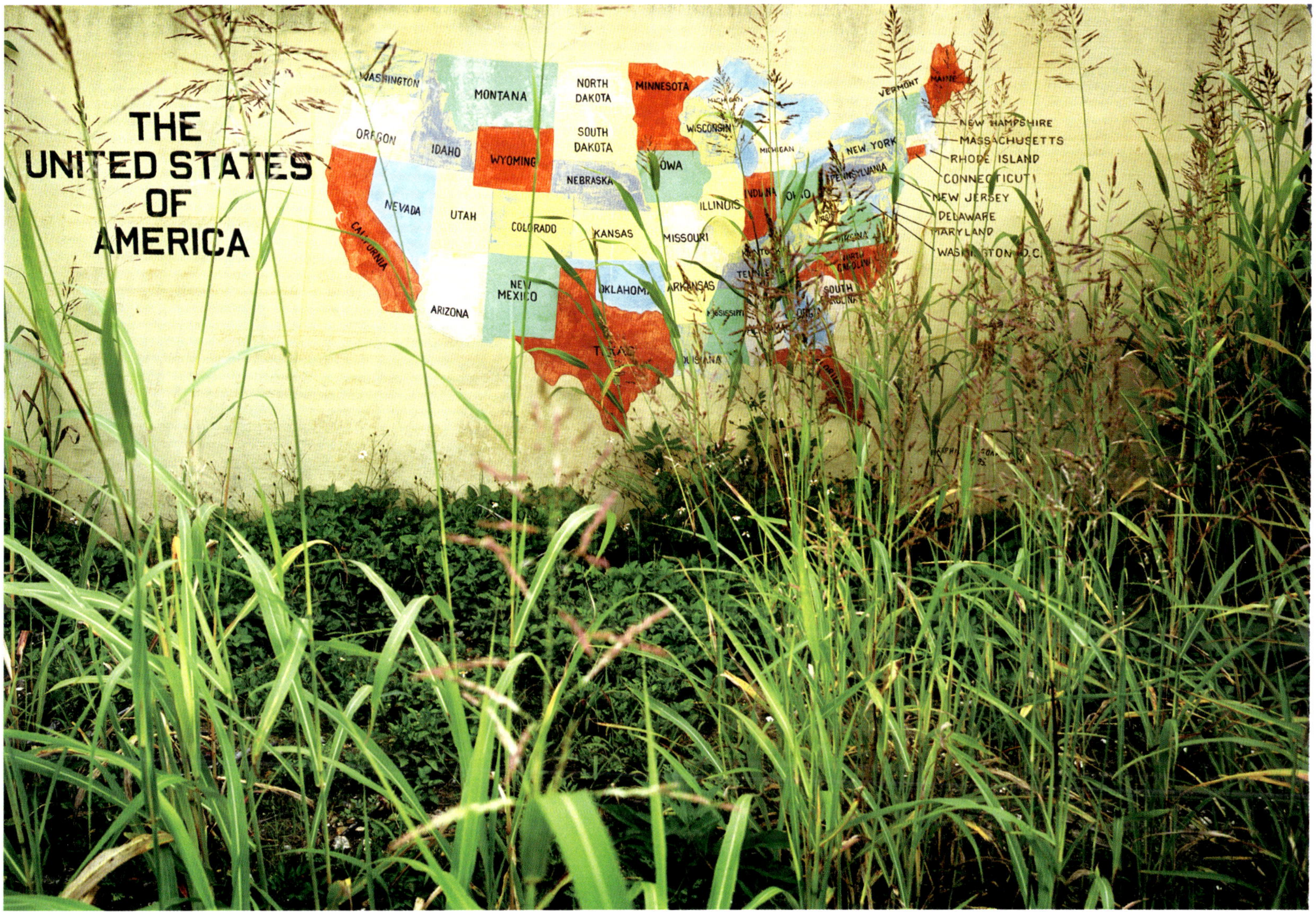
THE
UNITED STATES
OF
AMERICA
WASHINGTON
MONTANA
NORTH
DAKOTA
MINNESOTA
VERMONT
MAINE
OREGON
IDAHO
WYOMING
SOUTH
DAKOTA
WISCONSIN
NEW YORK
NEW HAMPSHIRE
MASSACHUSETTS
RHODE ISLAND
NEBRASKA
IOWA
CONNECTICUT
NEVADA
UTAH
ILLINOIS
NEW JERSEY
DELAWARE
COLORADO
KANSAS
MISSOURI
MARYLAND
WASHINGTON D.C.
OKLAHOMA
ARKANSAS
NEW
MEXICO
ARIZONA
SOUTH
CAROLINA

11. ST. MAURICE AVENUE

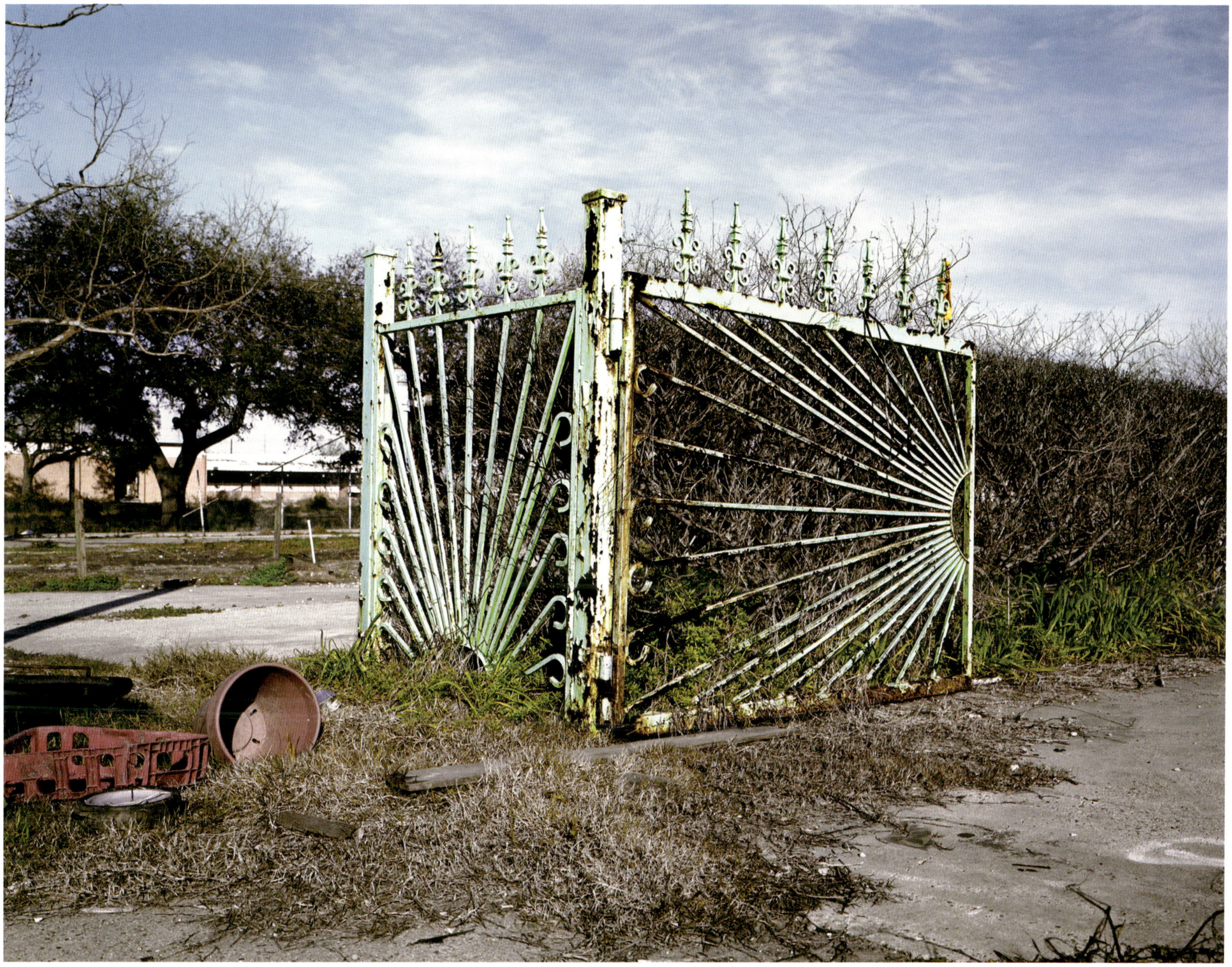

12. PHIPPS INN

ALABO STREET

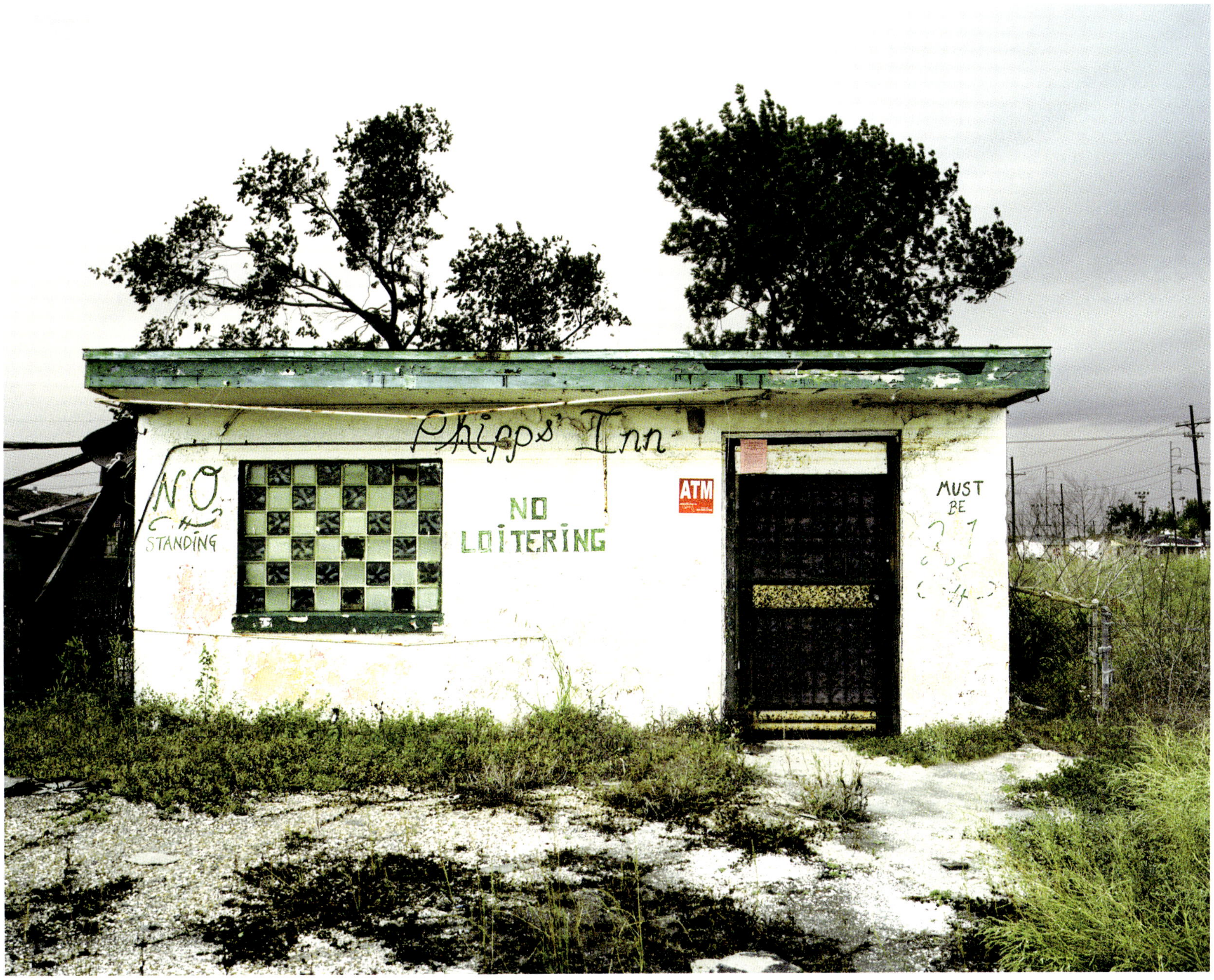
Phipps' Inn
NO
STANDING
NO
LOITERING
ATM
MUST
BE

13. CAFFIN AVENUE

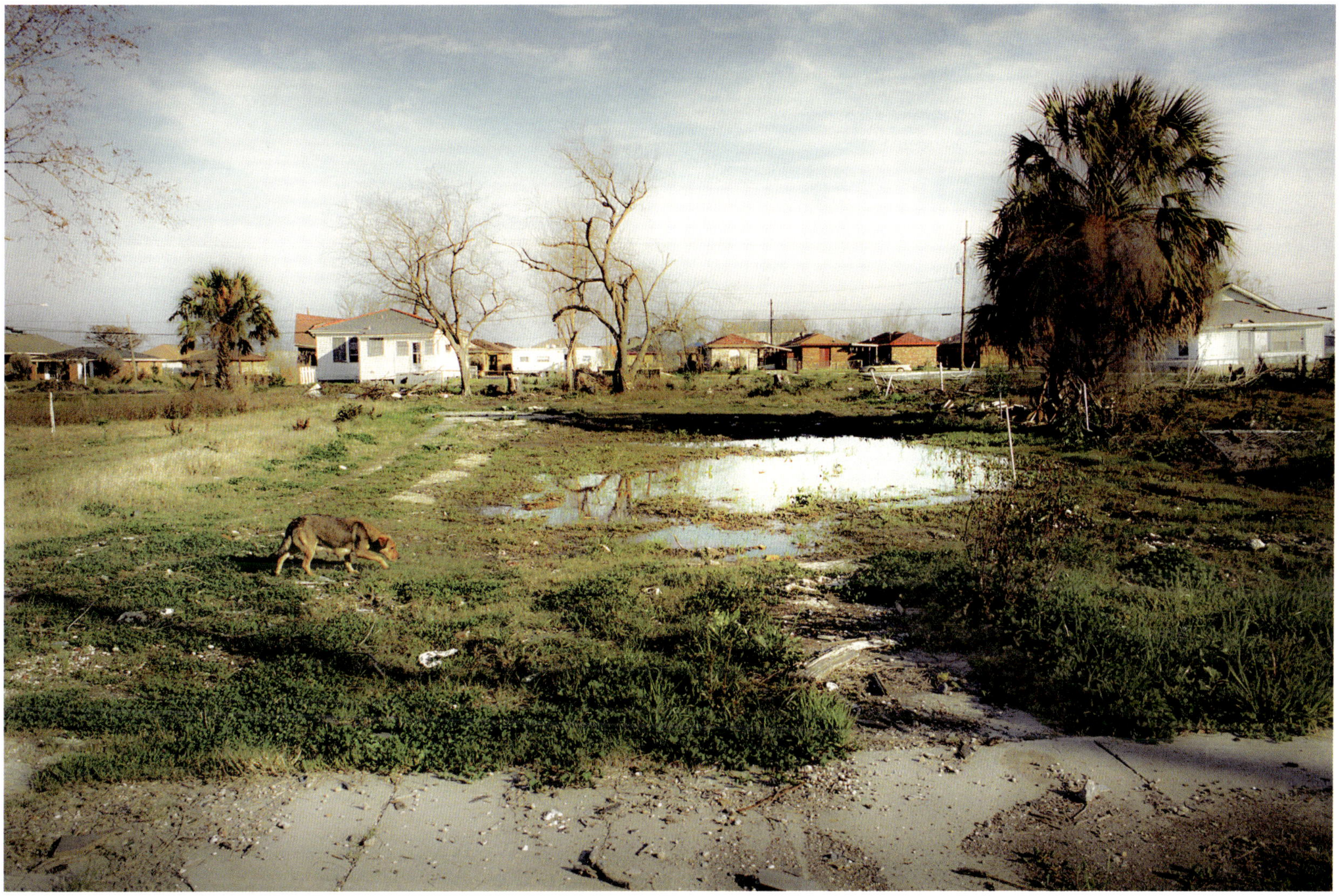

14. ROFFIGNAC STREET

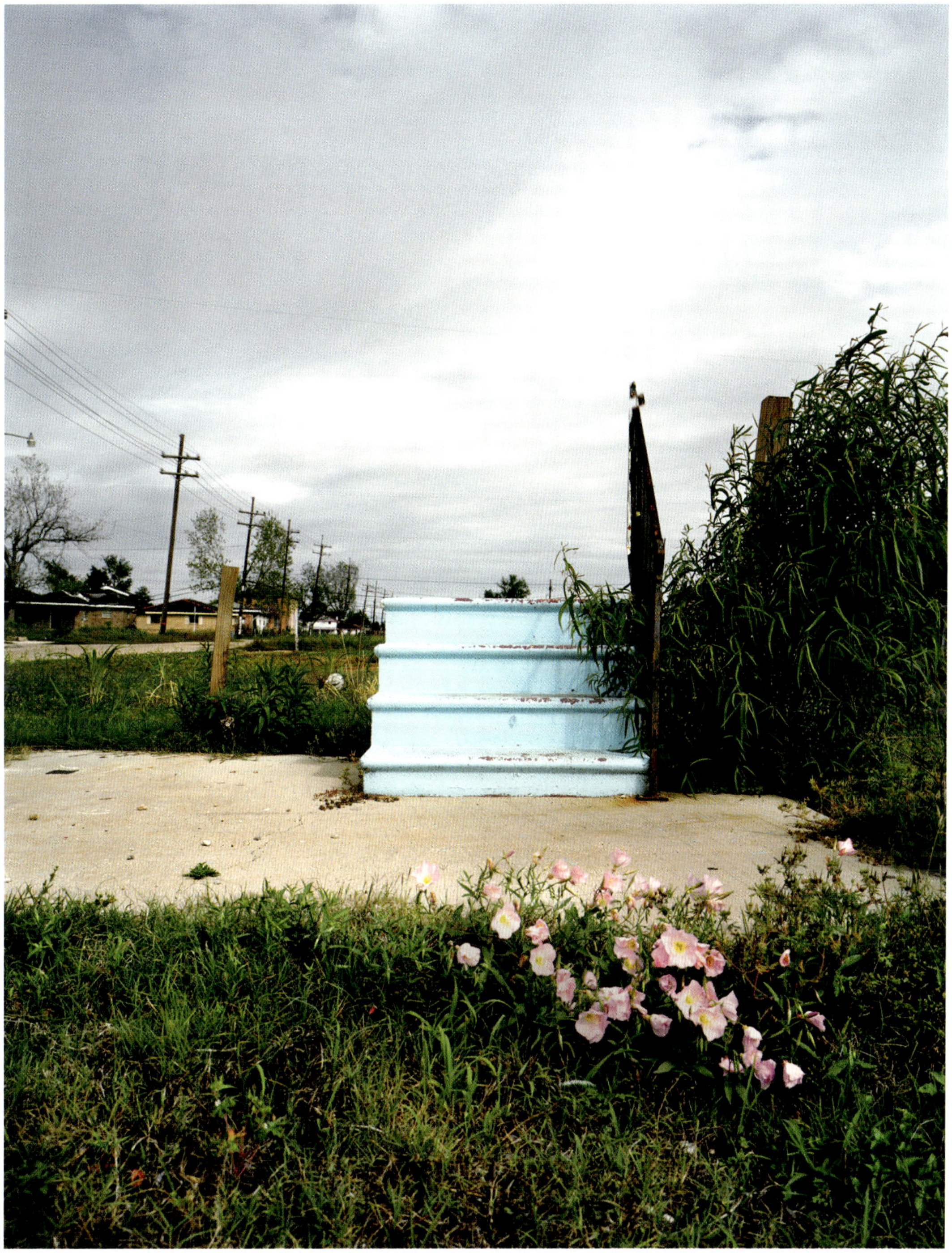

15. CHURCH OF THE LIVING GOD

CHARBONNET STREET

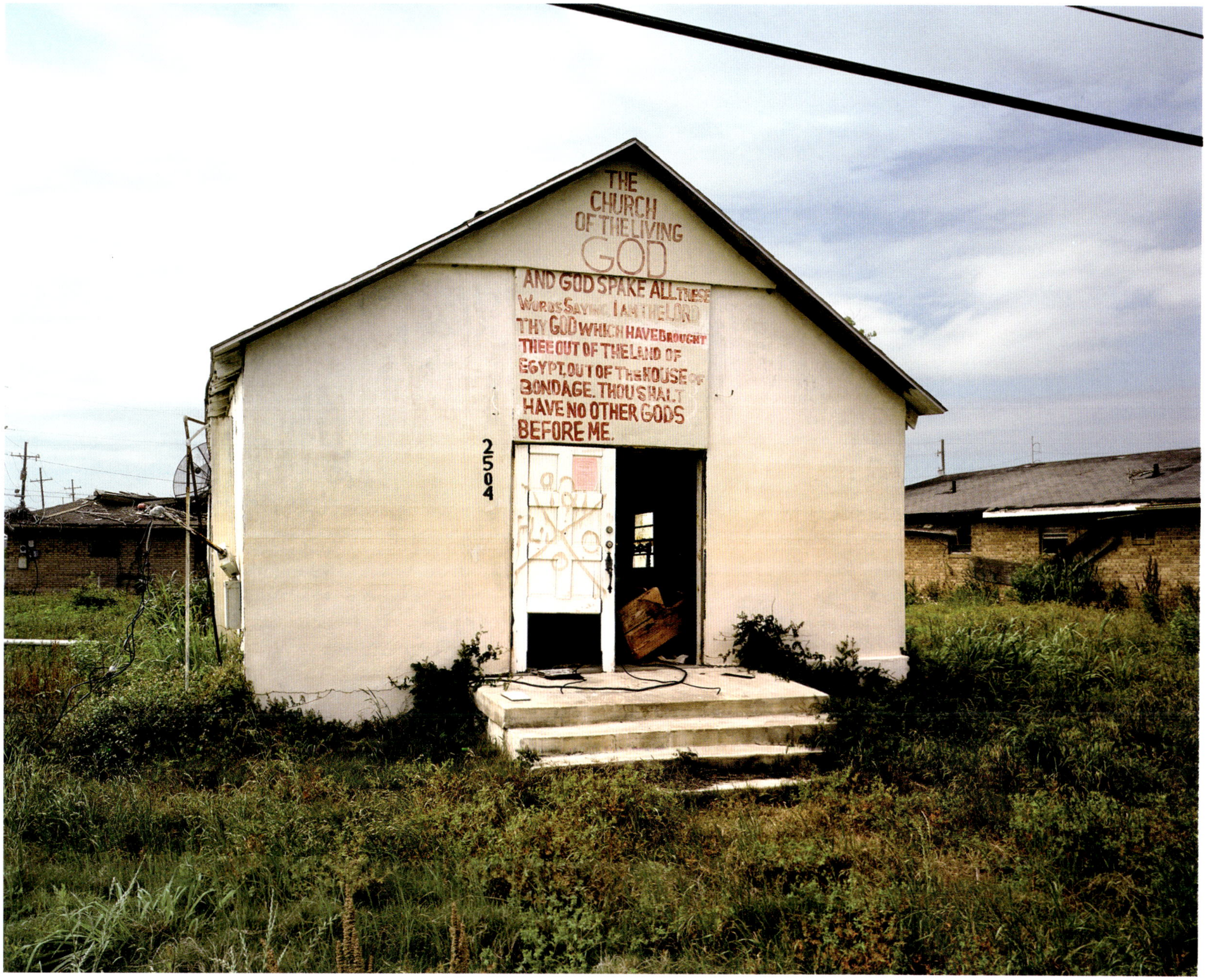
THE CHURCH OF THE LIVING GOD
AND GOD SPAKE ALL THESE WORDS SAYING I AM THE LORD THY GOD WHICH HAVE BROUGHT THEE OUT OF THE LAND OF EGYPT, OUT OF THE HOUSE OF BONDAGE. THOU SHALT HAVE NO OTHER GODS BEFORE ME.
2504

16. RECEPTION HALL
ST. MAURICE AVENUE

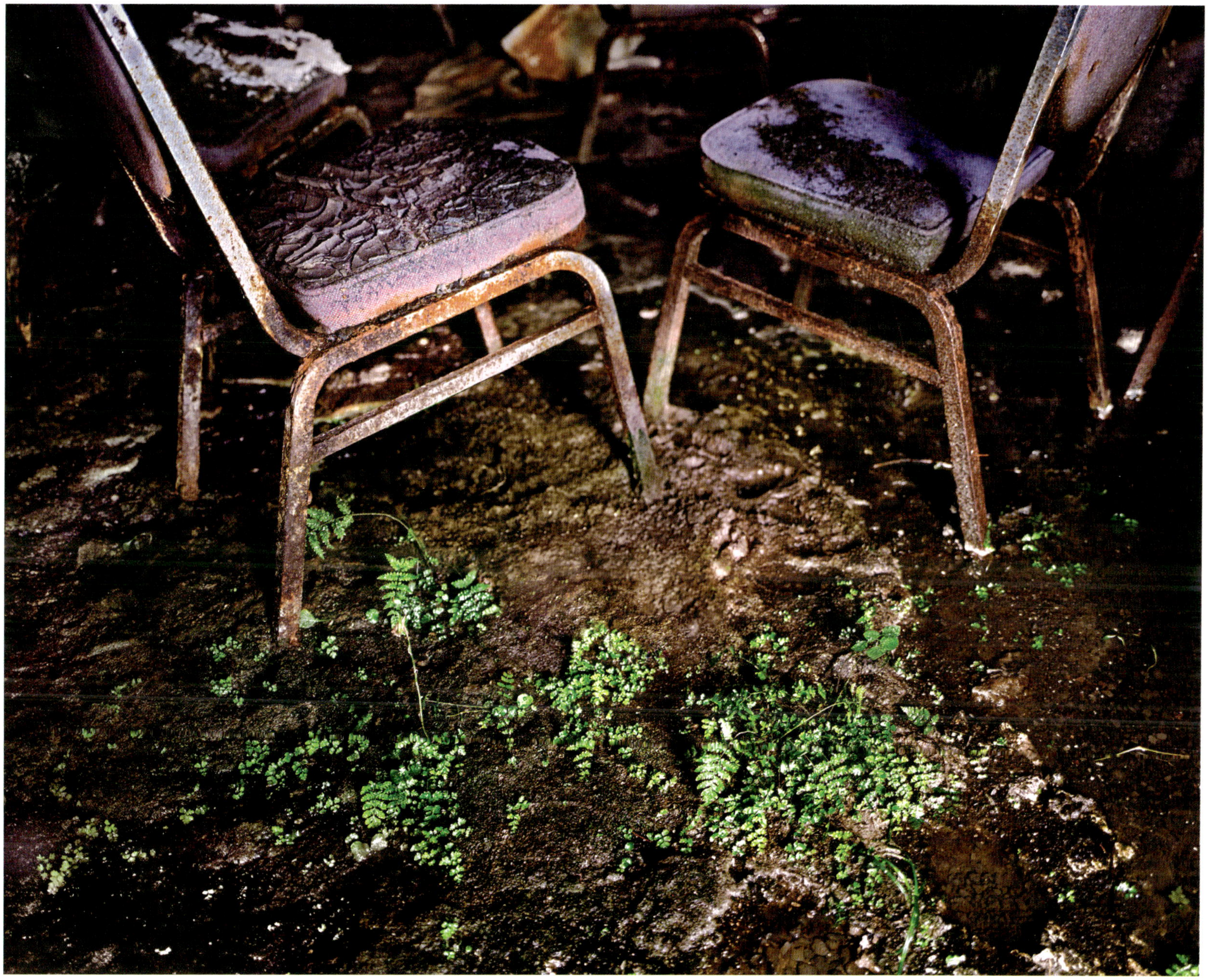

17. ALABO STREET

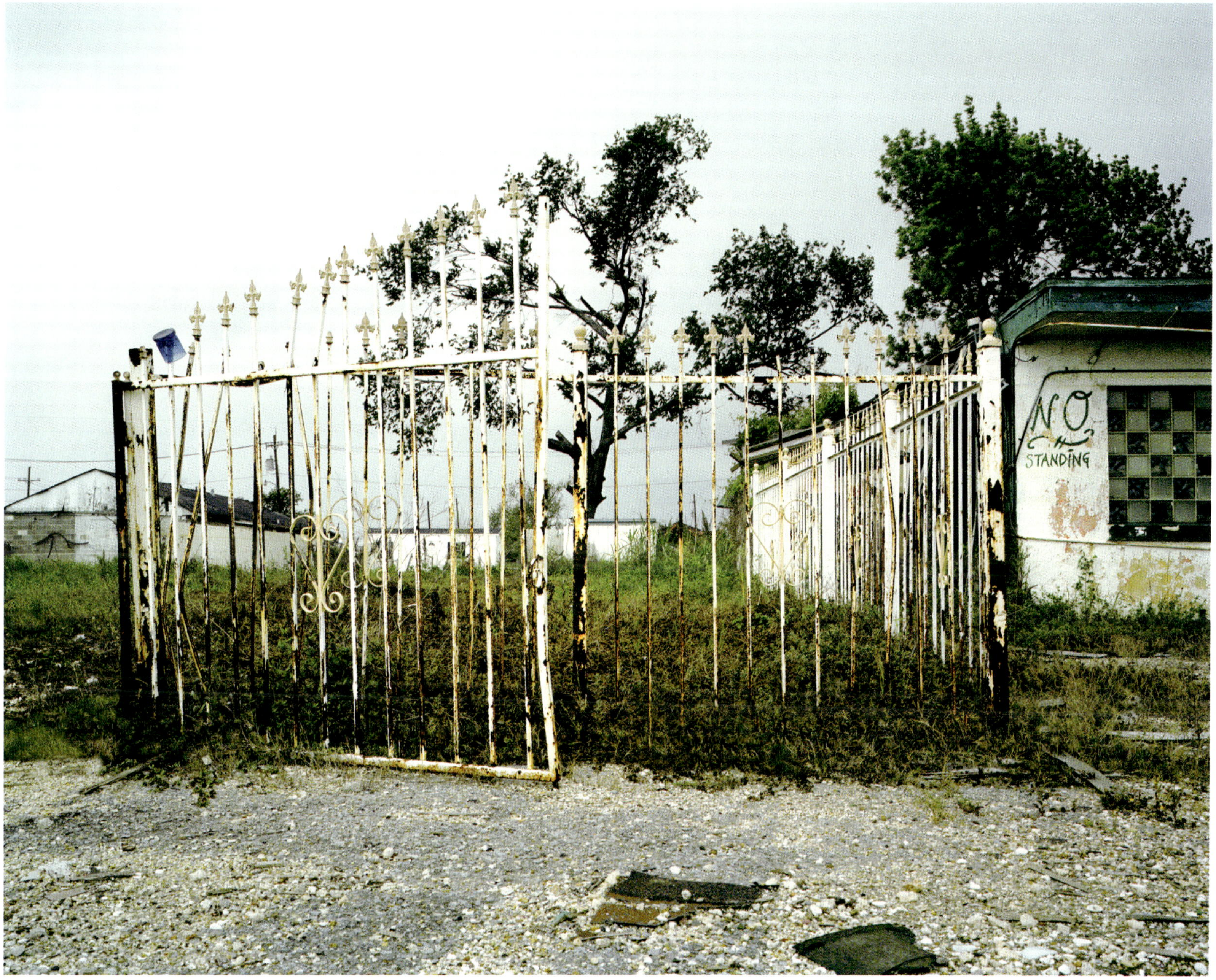
NO
STANDING

18. CHURCH OF THE LIVING GOD

CHARBONNET STREET

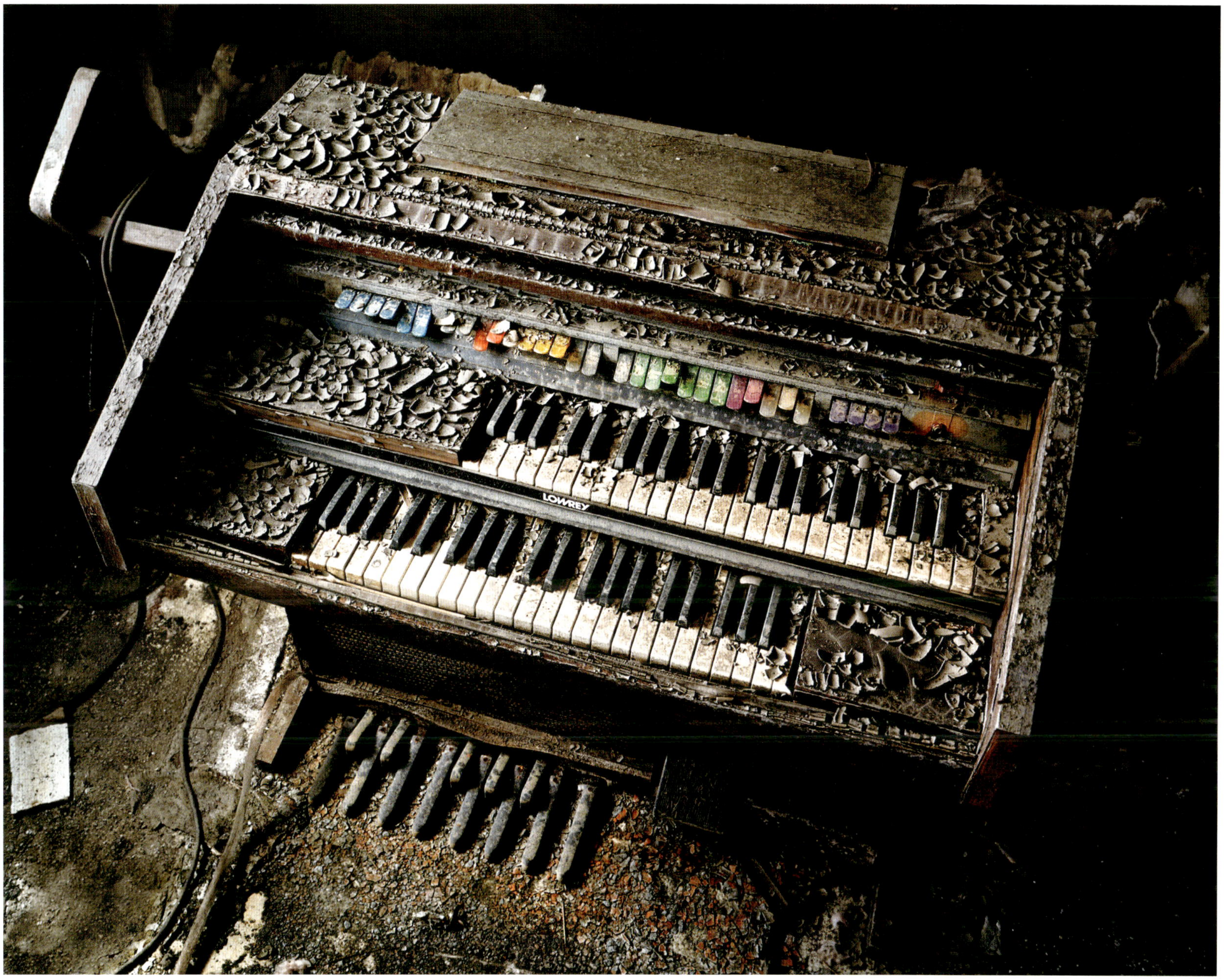
LOWREY

19. NORTH VILLERE STREET

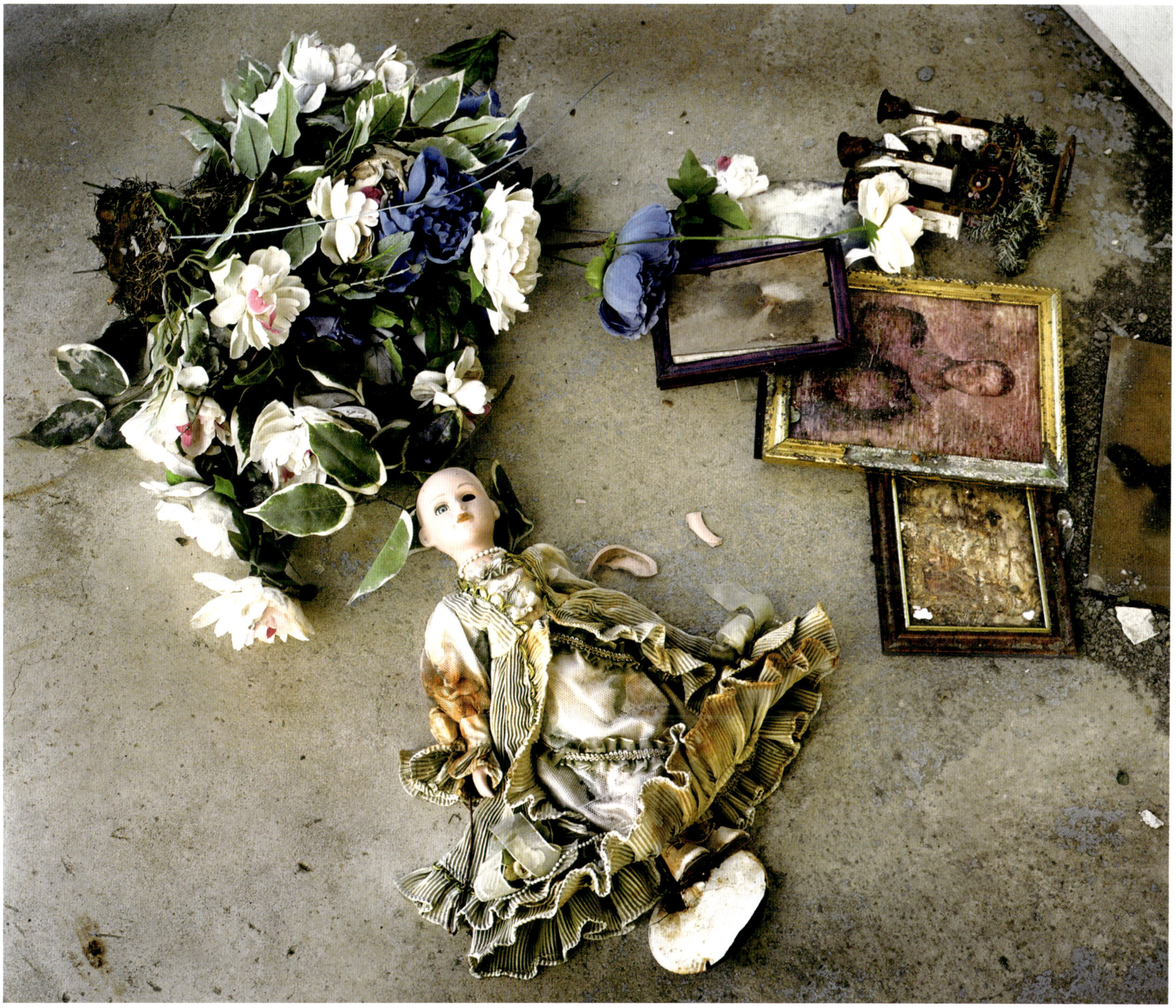

20. JOHNSON STREET

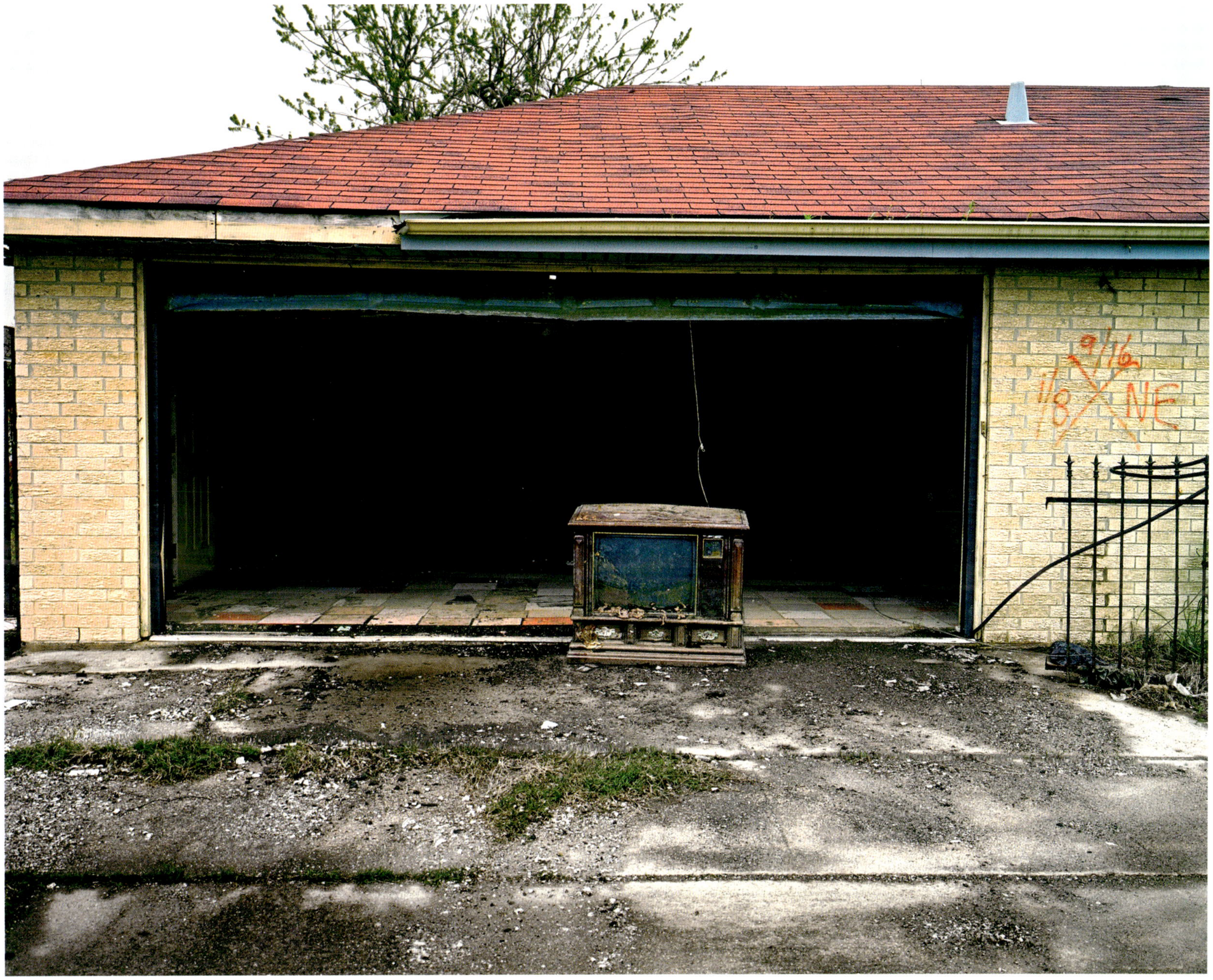
9/16
1/8
NE

21. LOUIS ARMSTRONG ELEMENTARY SCHOOL

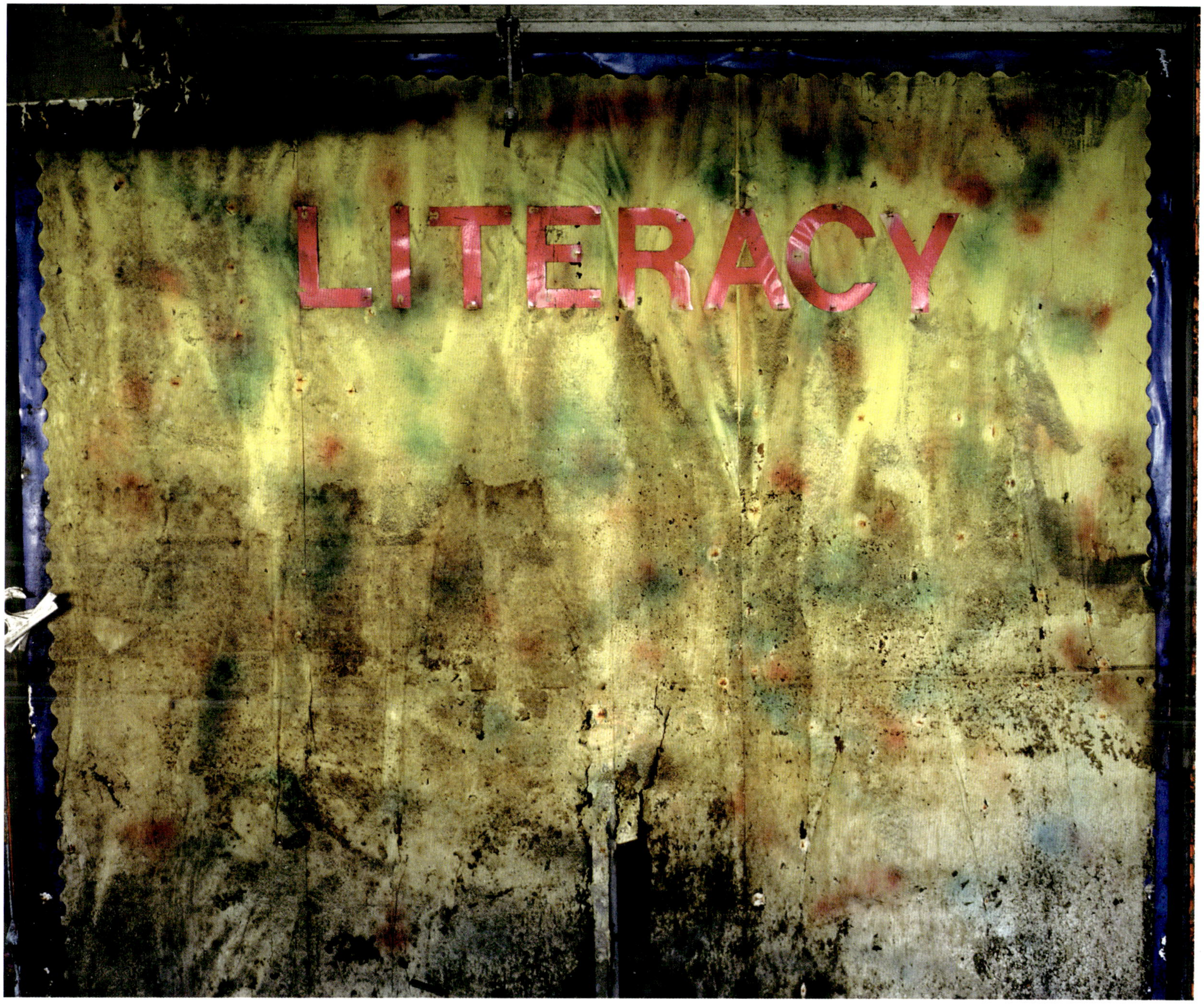
LITERACY

22. DORGENOIS STREET

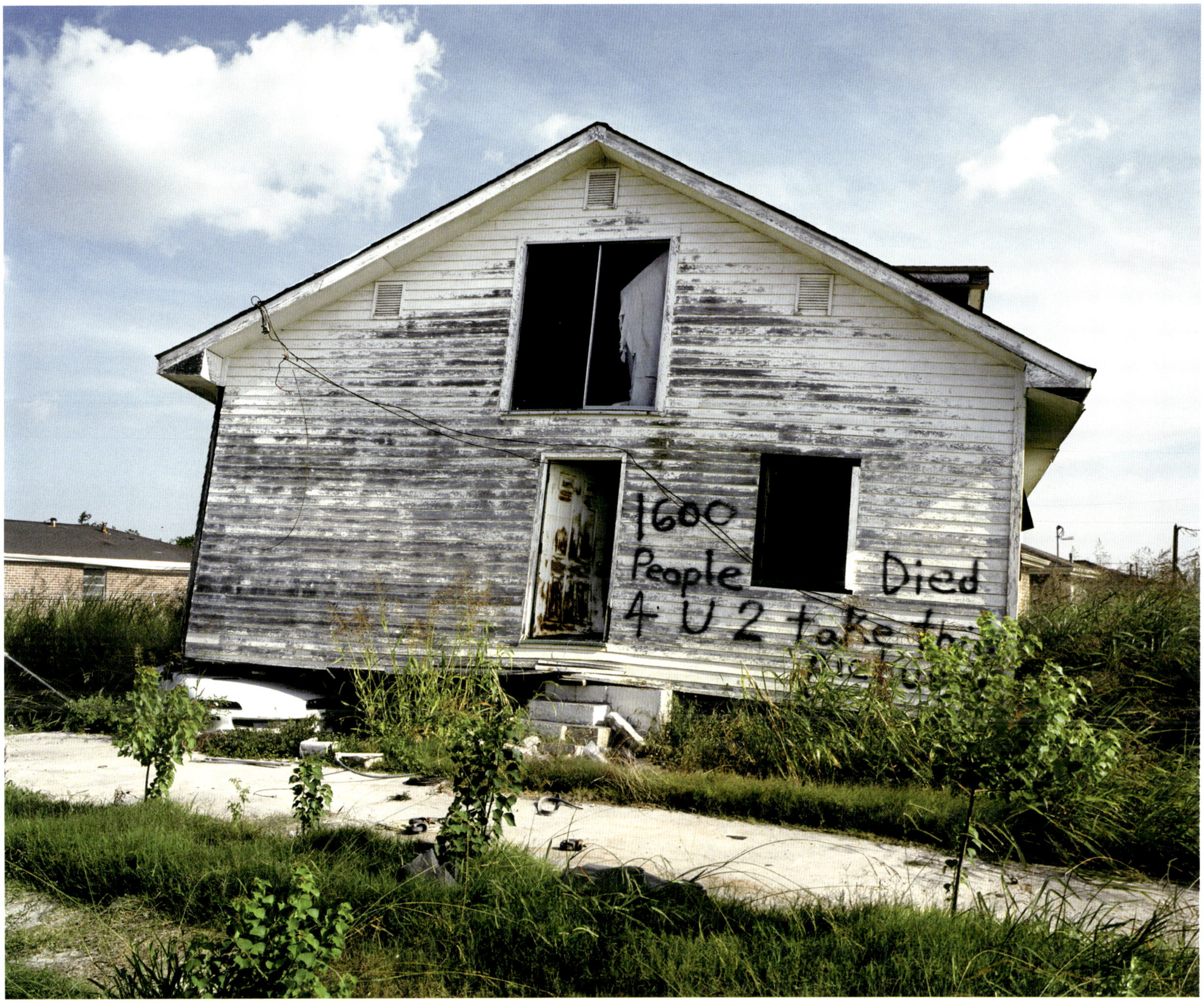
1600
People Died
4 U 2 take

23. LIZARDI STREET

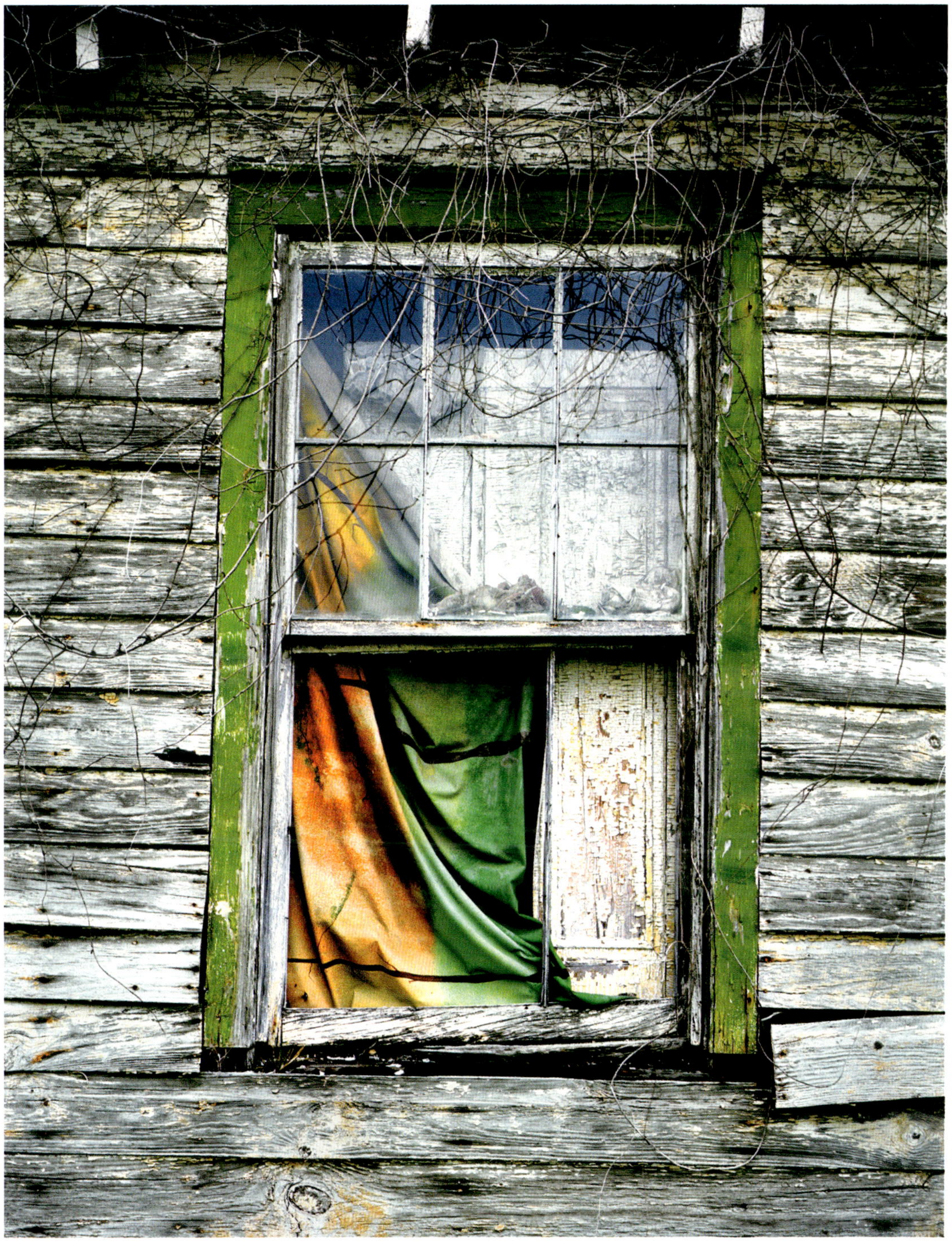

24. ST. ROSE MISSIONARY BAPTIST CHURCH

FORSTALL STREET

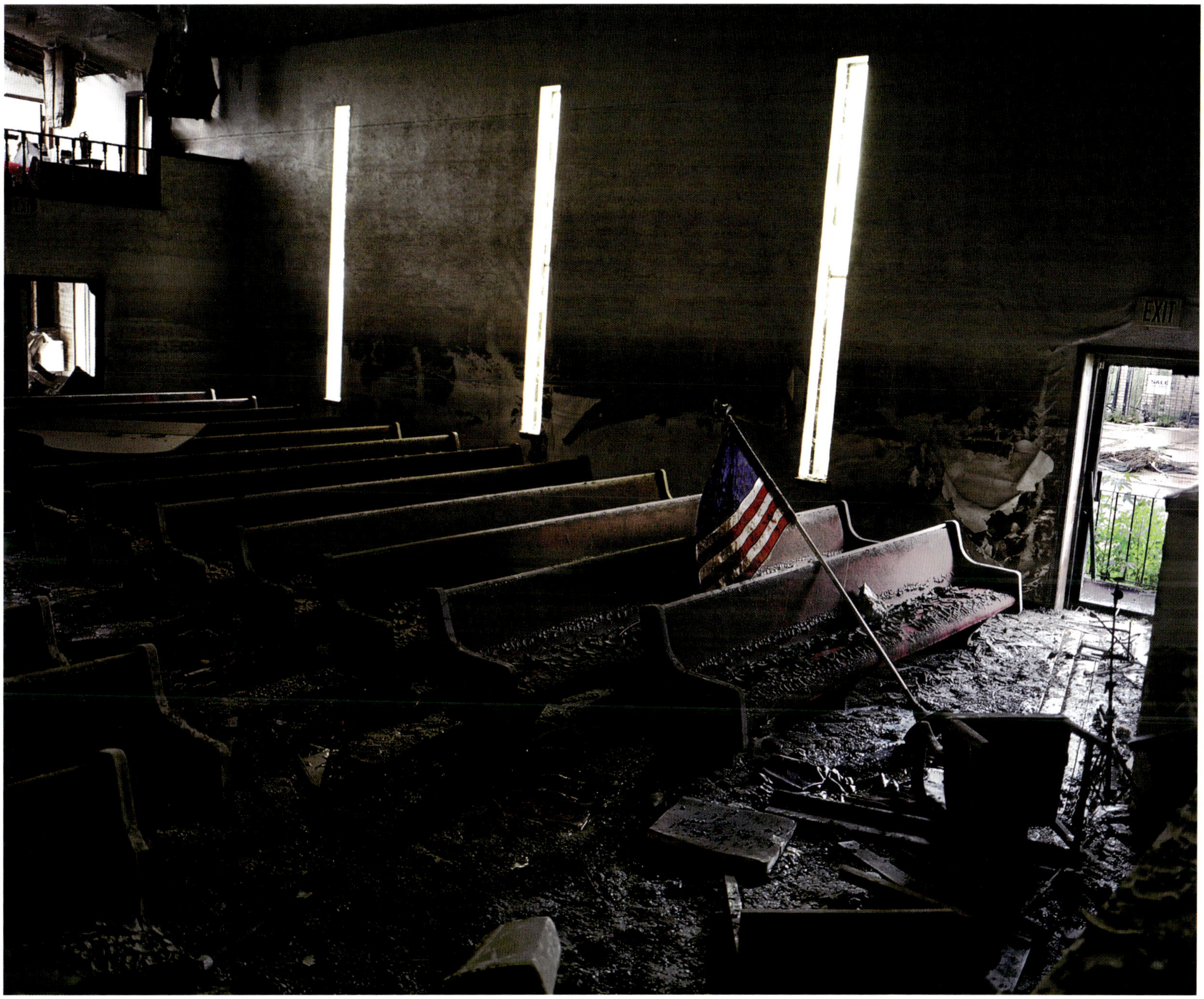
EXIT

25. BAGHDAD

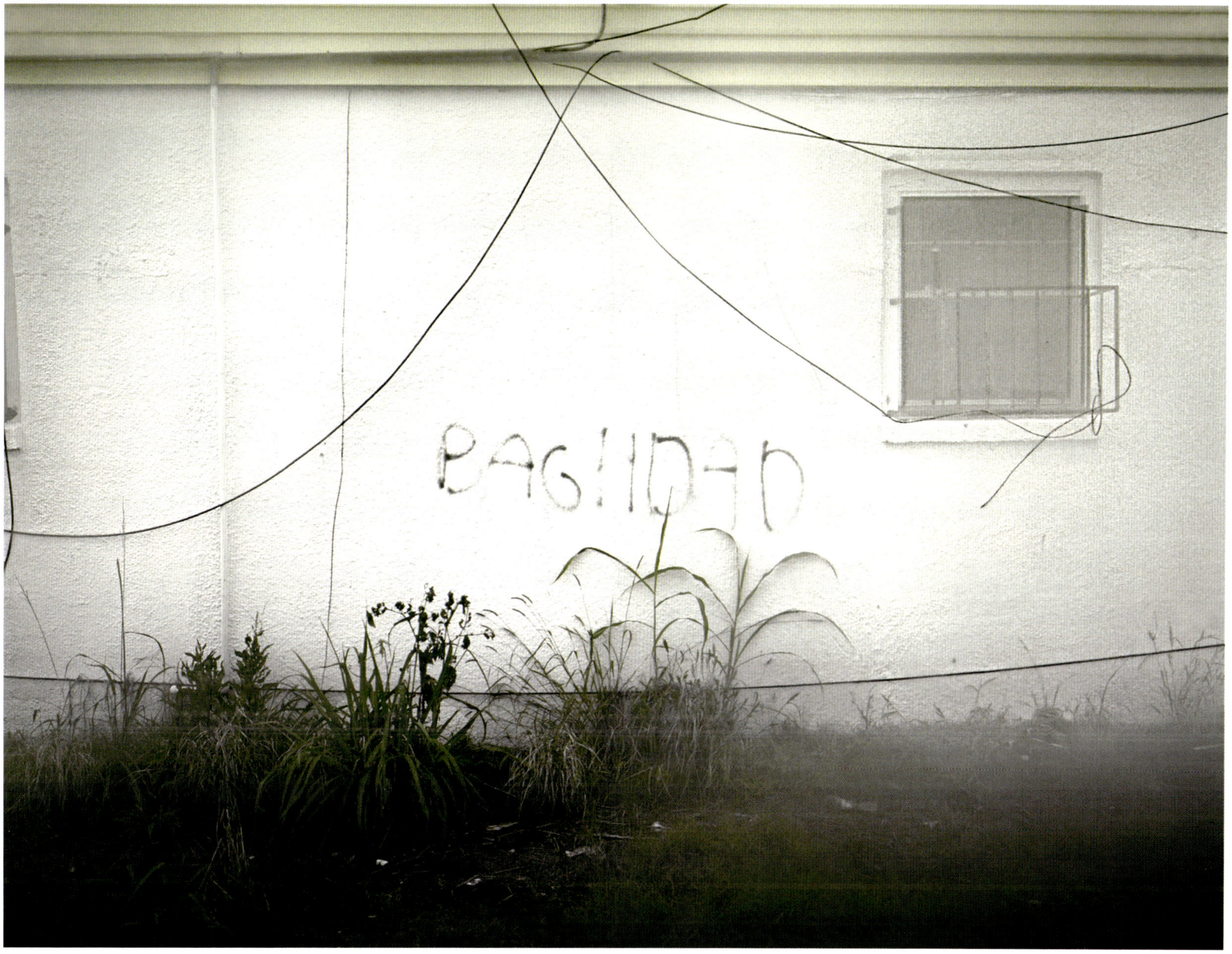
BAGHDAD

26. T & T LIQUOR AND GROCERY

GALVEZ STREET

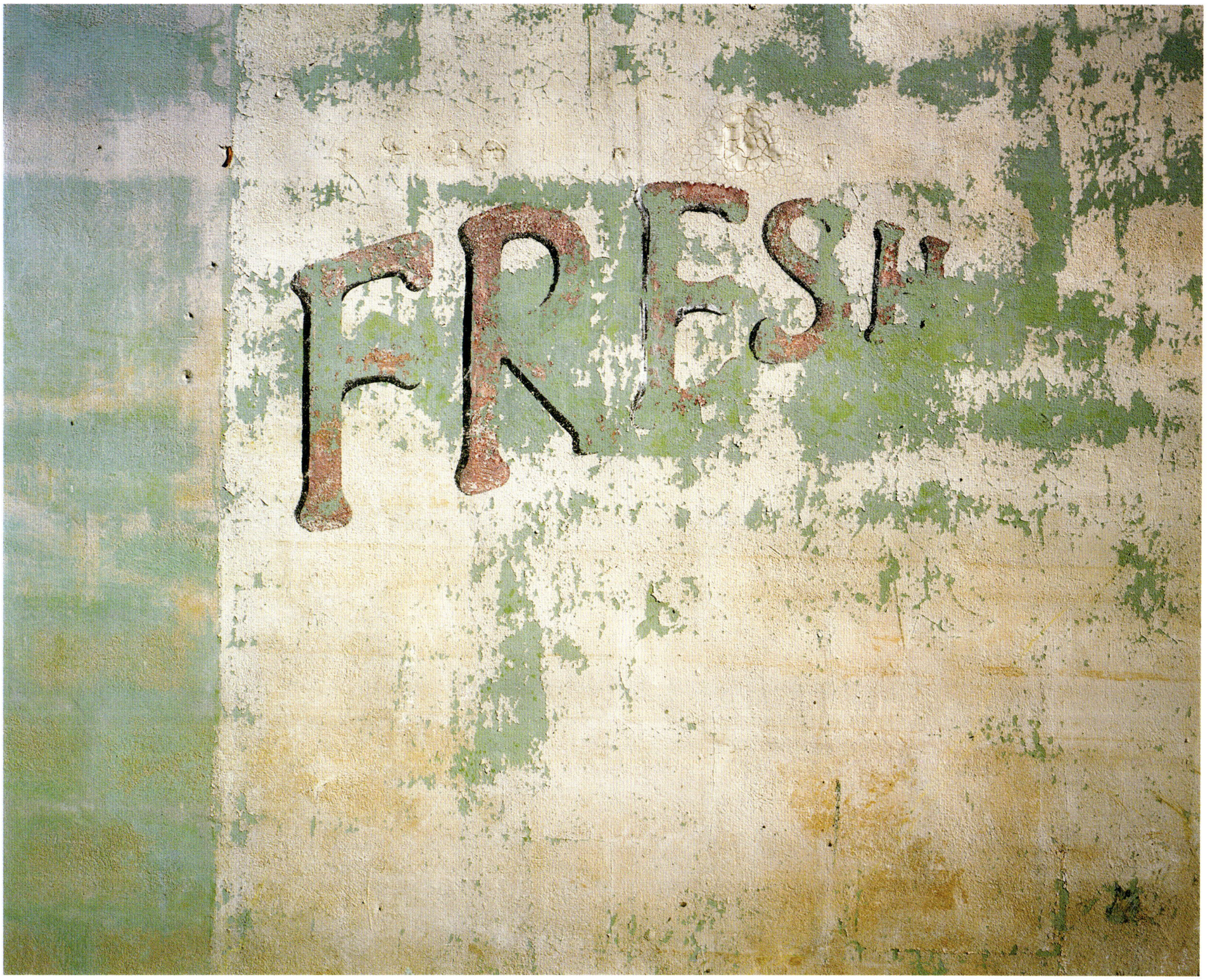
FRESH

27. LOUIS ARMSTRONG ELEMENTARY SCHOOL

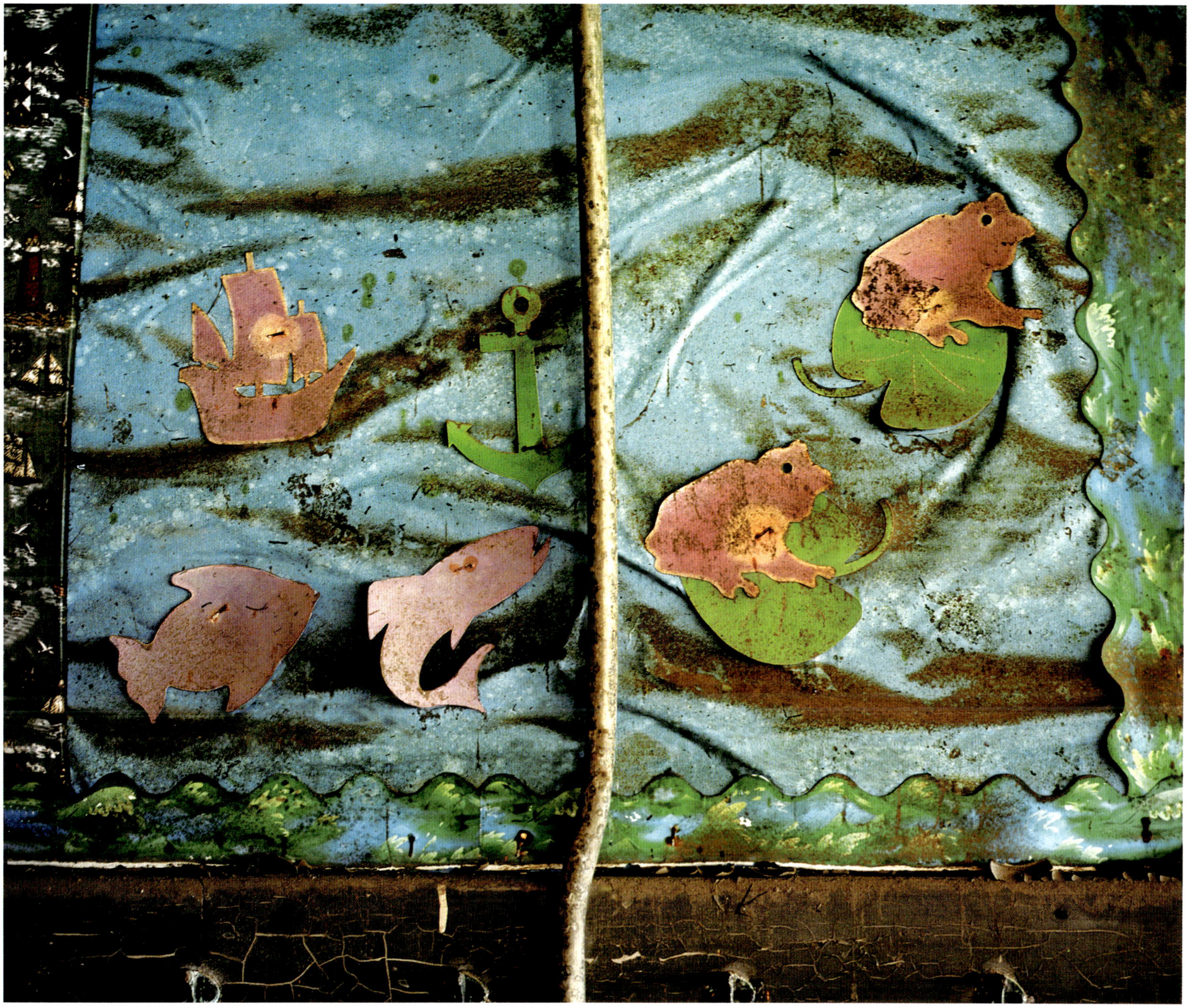

28. ROYAL STREET

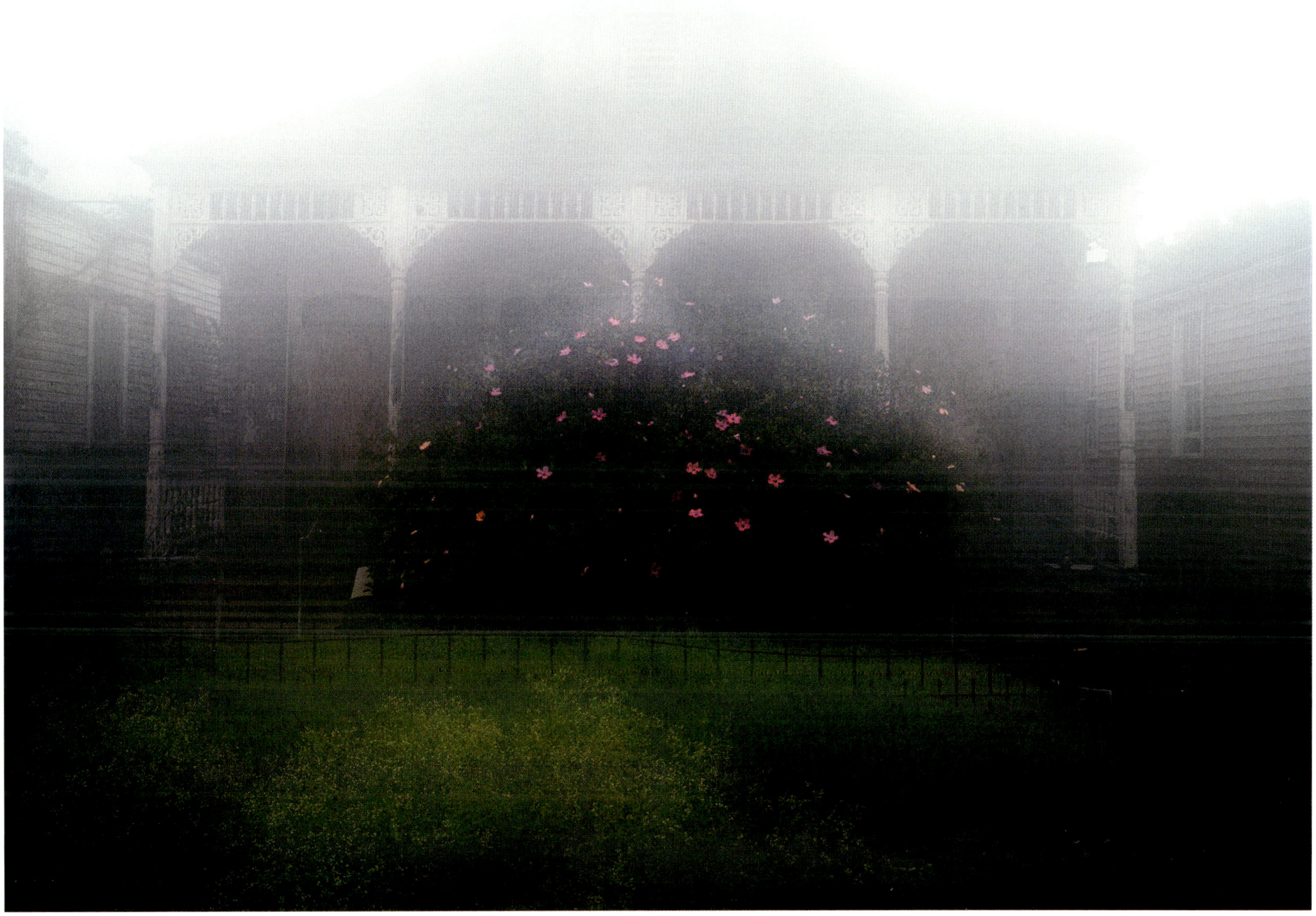

29. PILGRIM REST BAPTIST CHURCH

FLOOD STREET

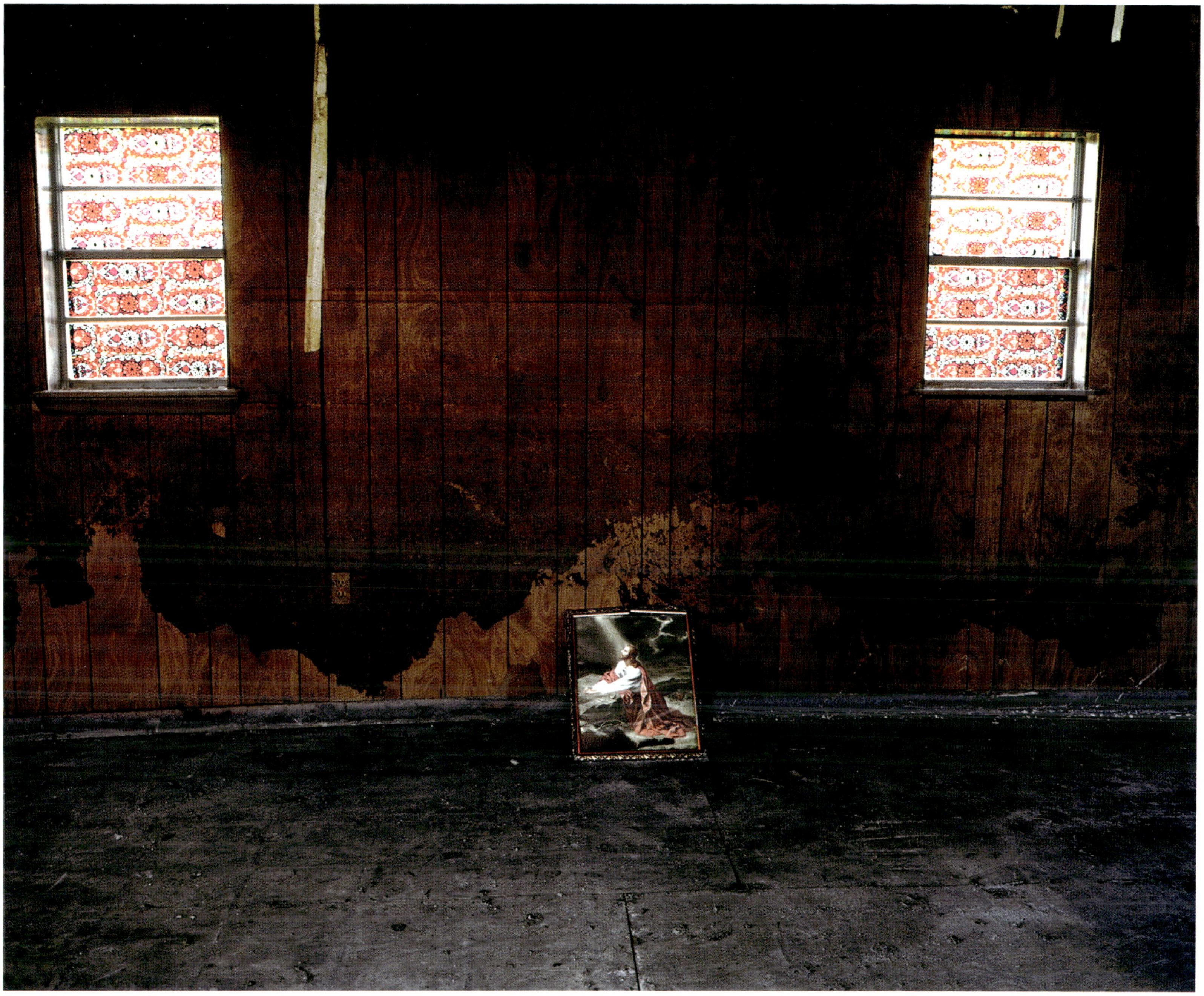

30. URQUHART STREET

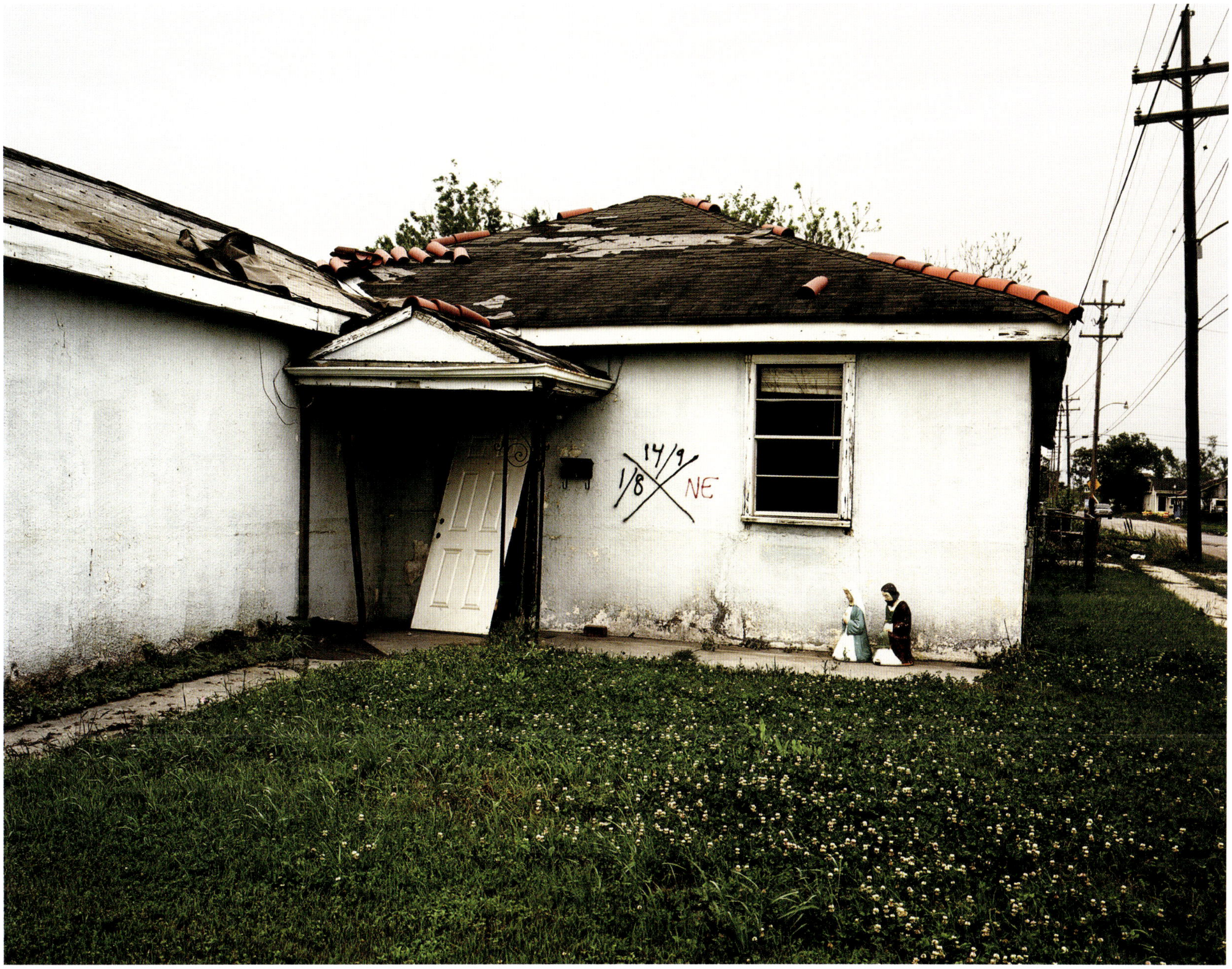
14/9
1/8
NE

31. TENNESSEE STREET

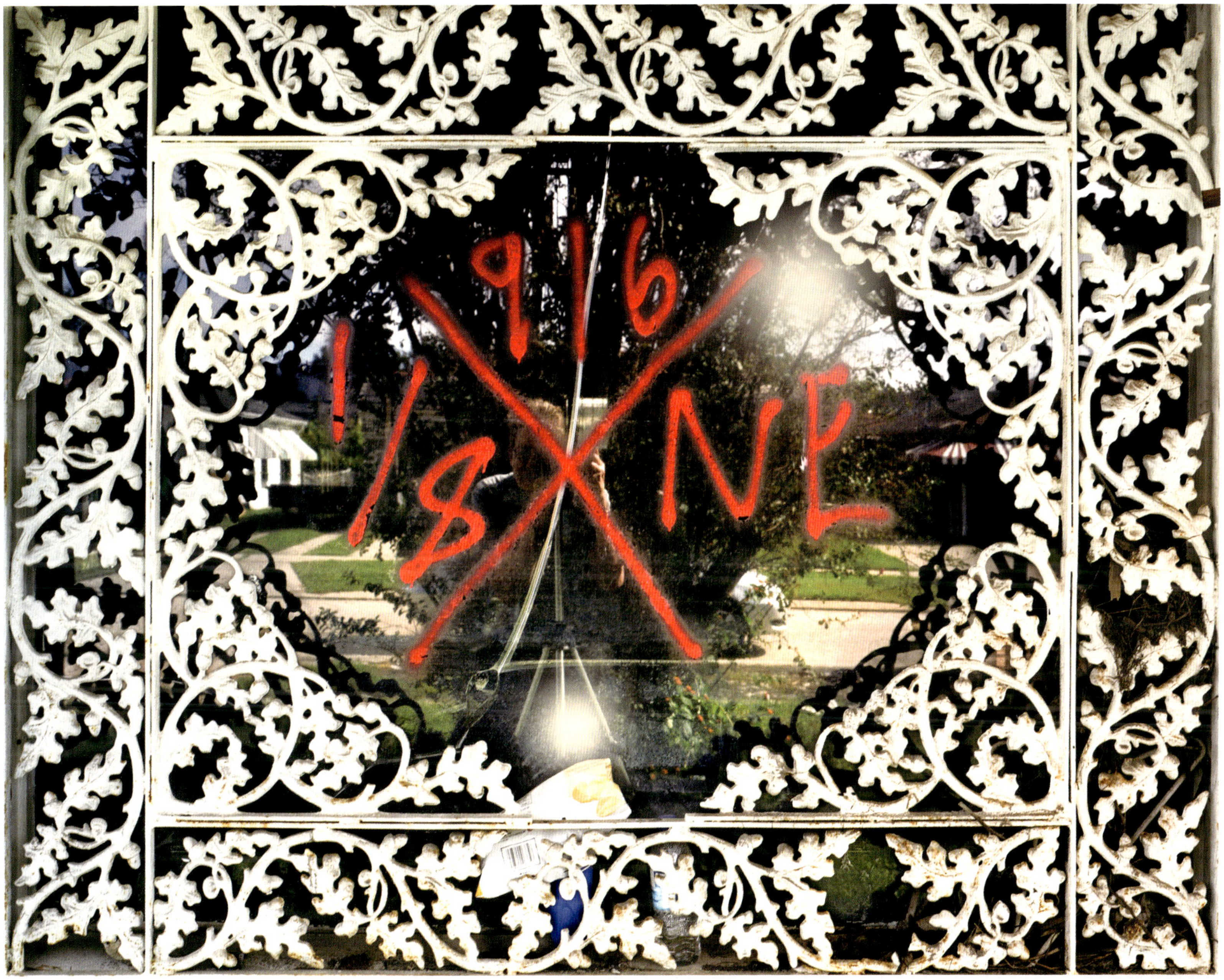

32. LOUIS ARMSTRONG ELEMENTARY SCHOOL

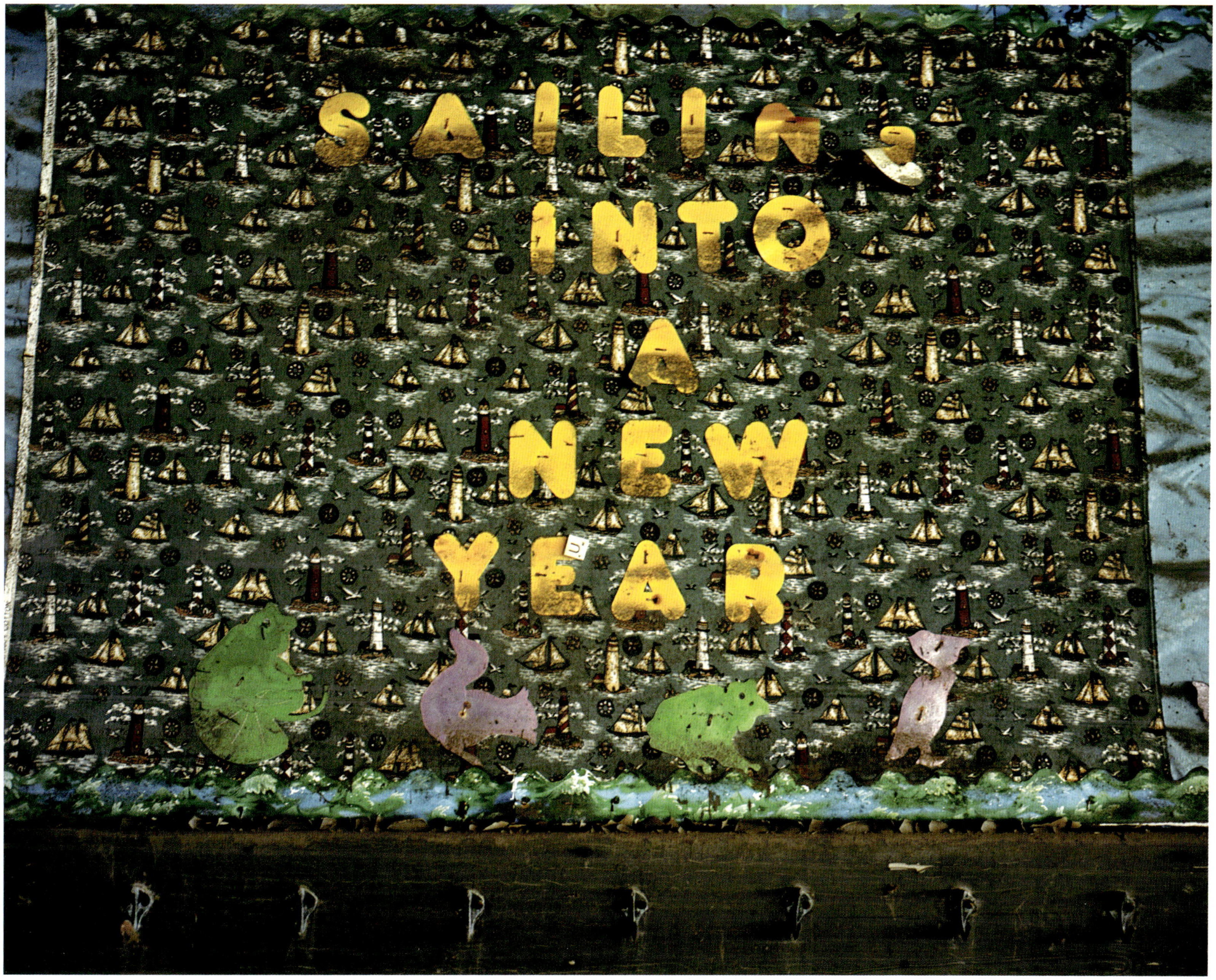
SAILING
INTO
A
NEW
YEAR

33. FATS DOMINO'S GARAGE DOOR

MARAIS STREET

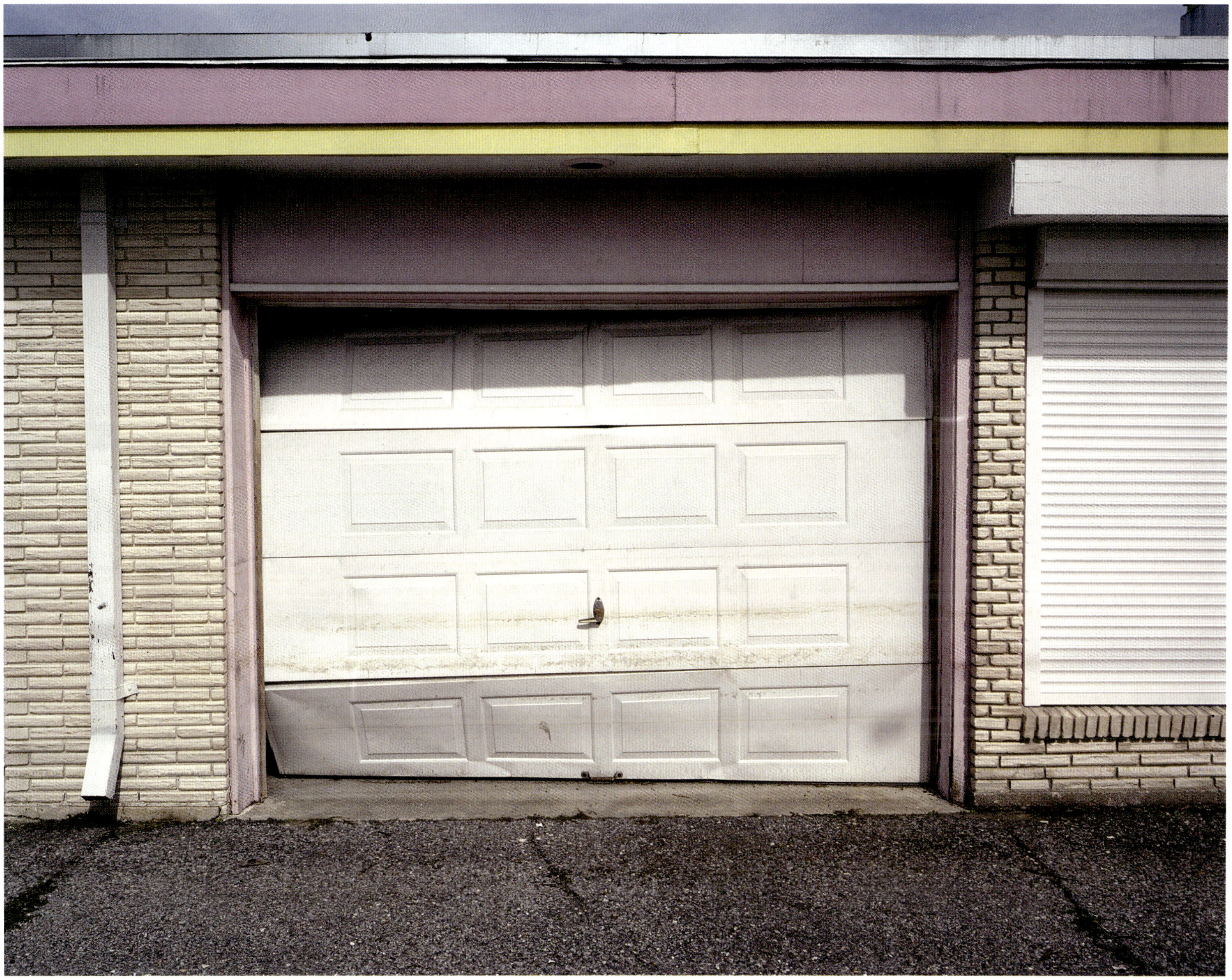

34. FLOOD STREET

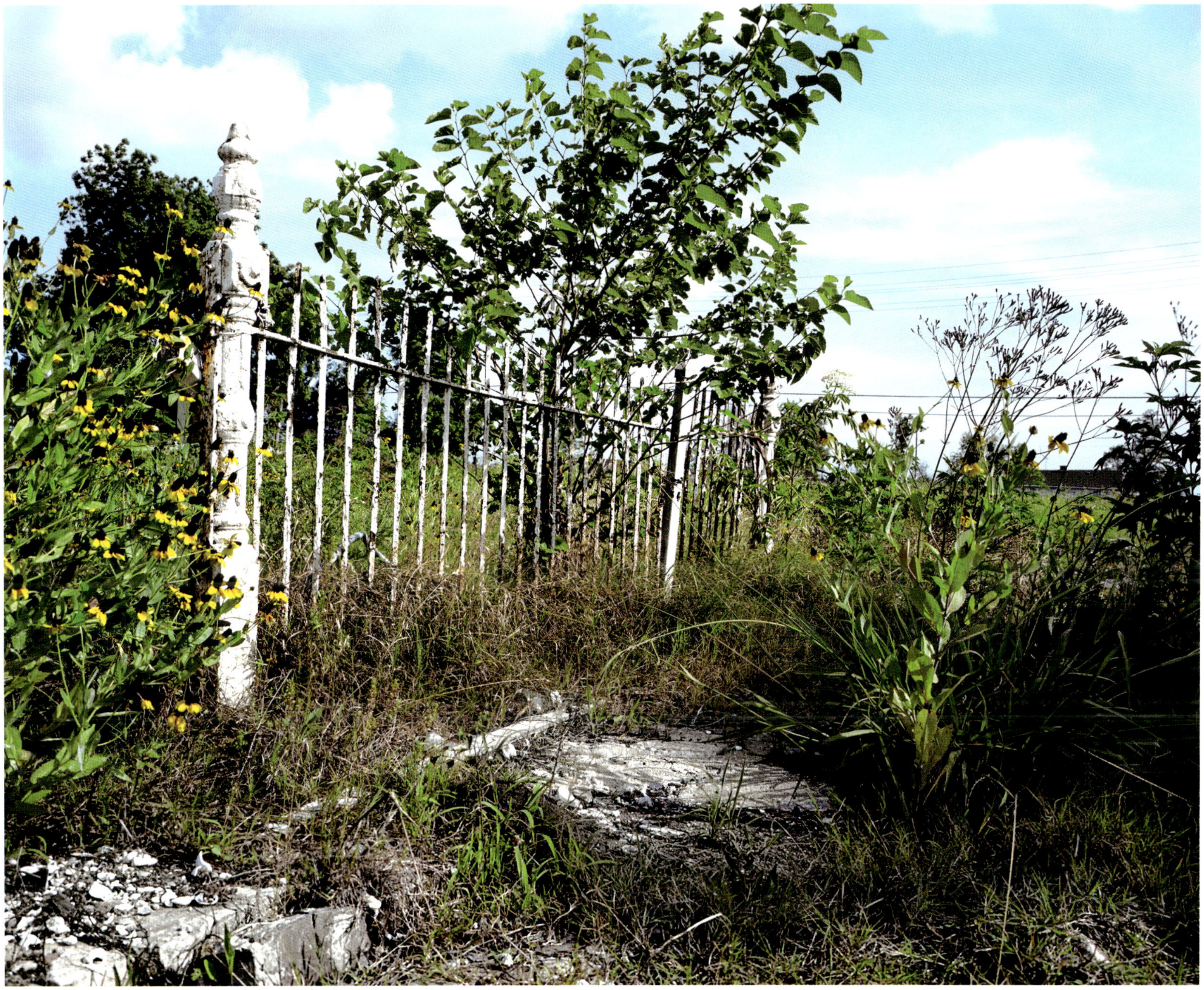

35. PSALM 91

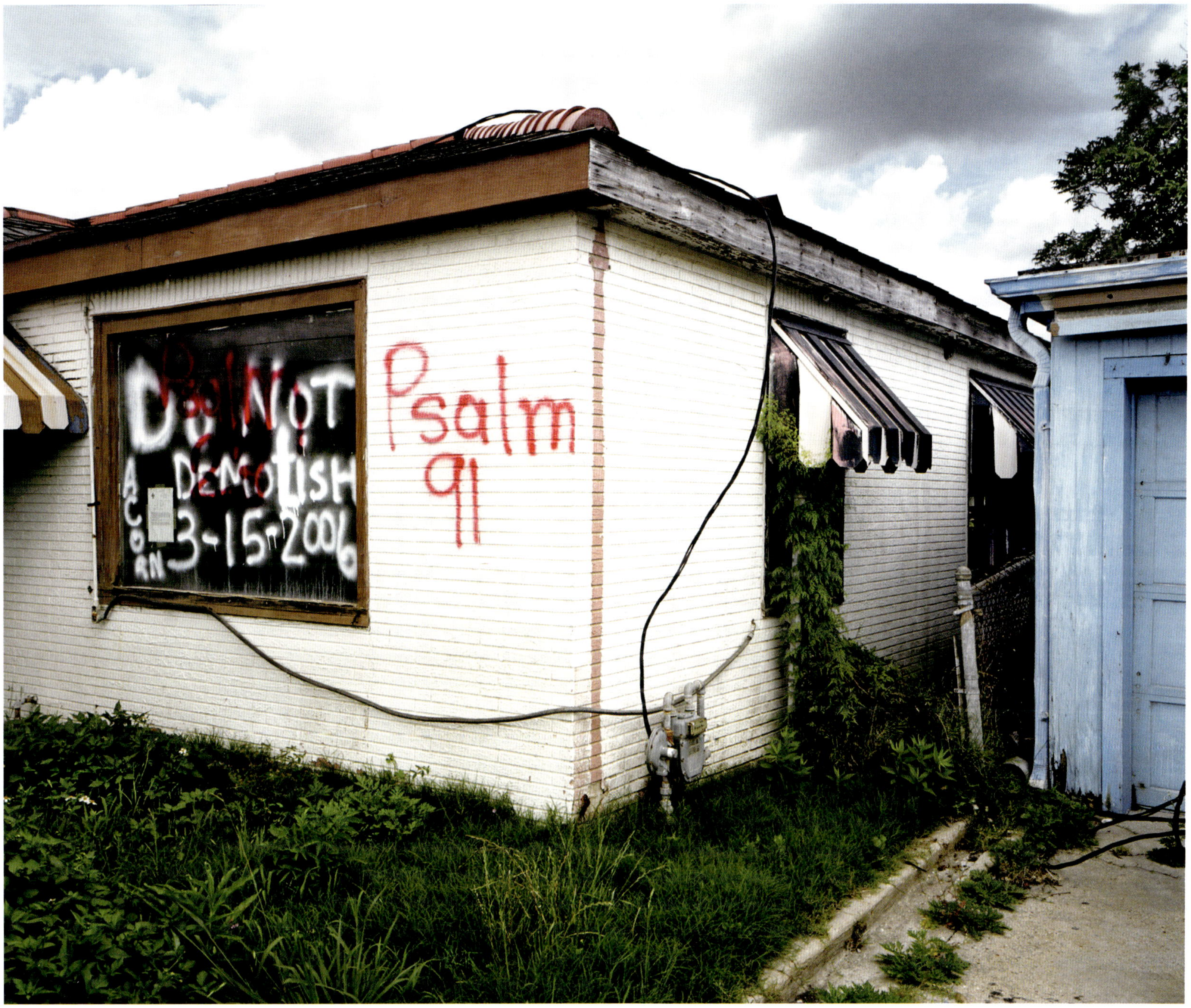
DO NOT
DEMOLISH
ACORN
3-15-2006
Psalm
91

36. TENNESSEE STREET

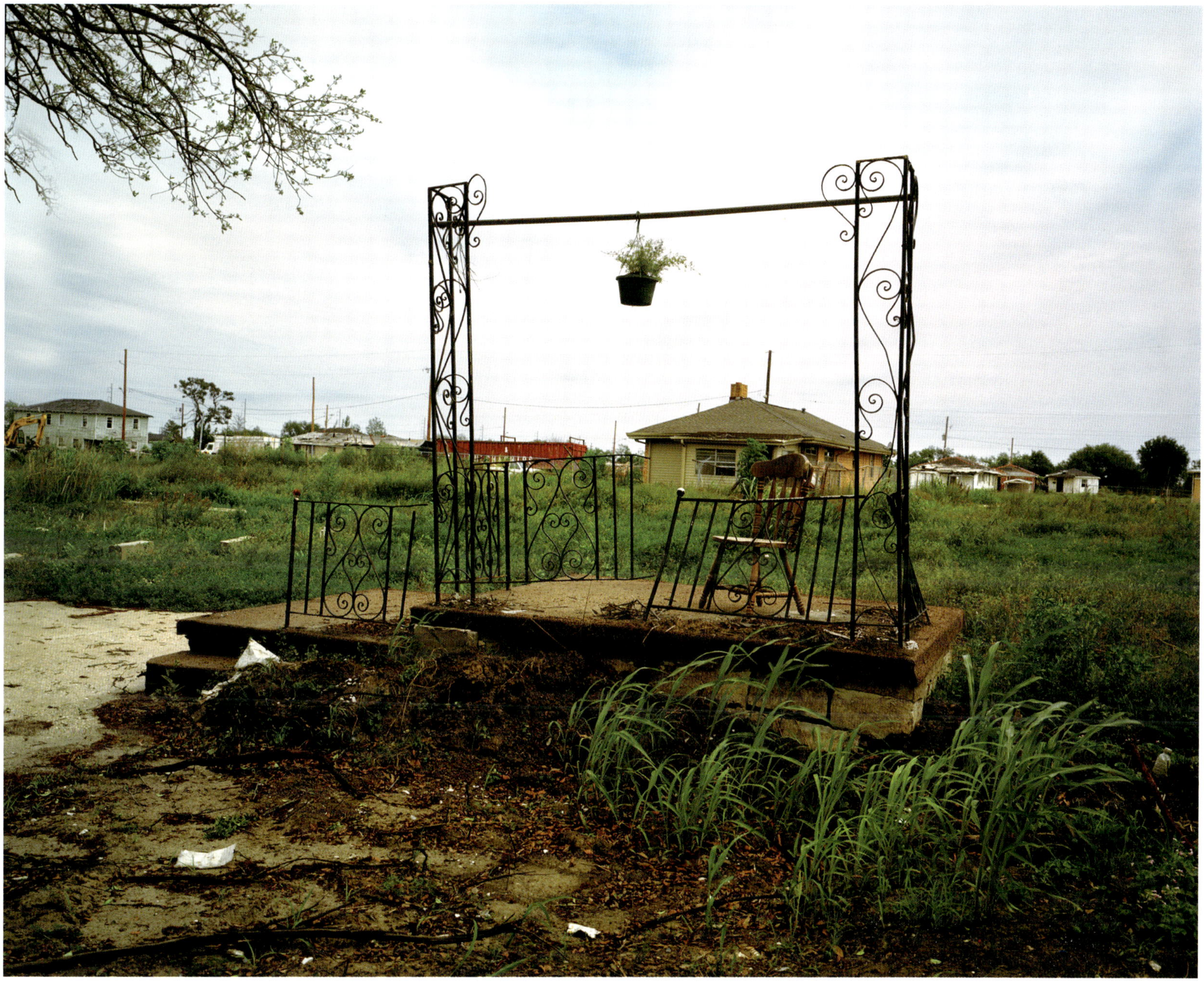

37. FOUNT, ISRAEL UNIVERSAL DIVINE CHURCH

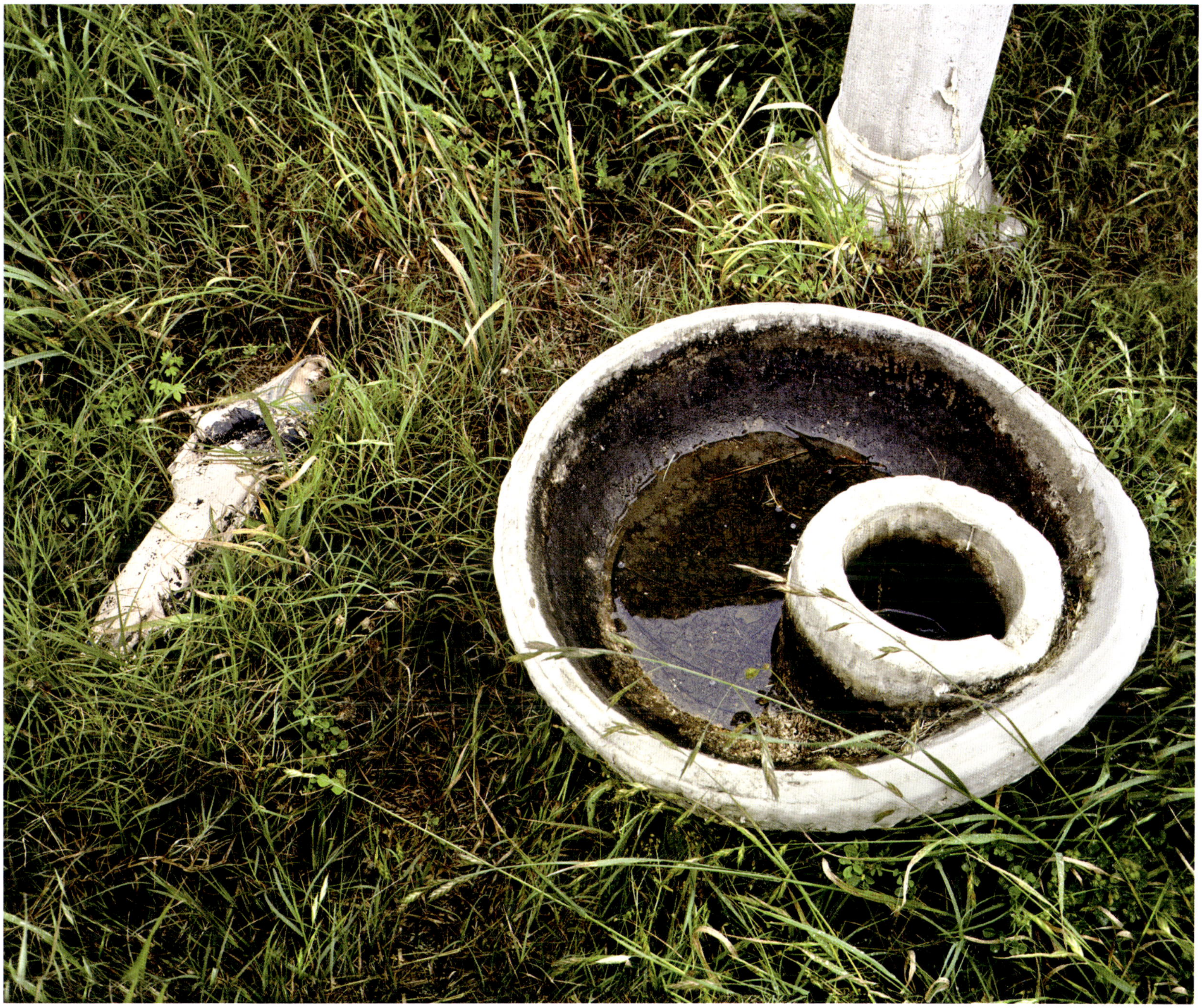

38. ST. ROSE MISSIONARY BAPTIST CHURCH
FORSTALL STREET

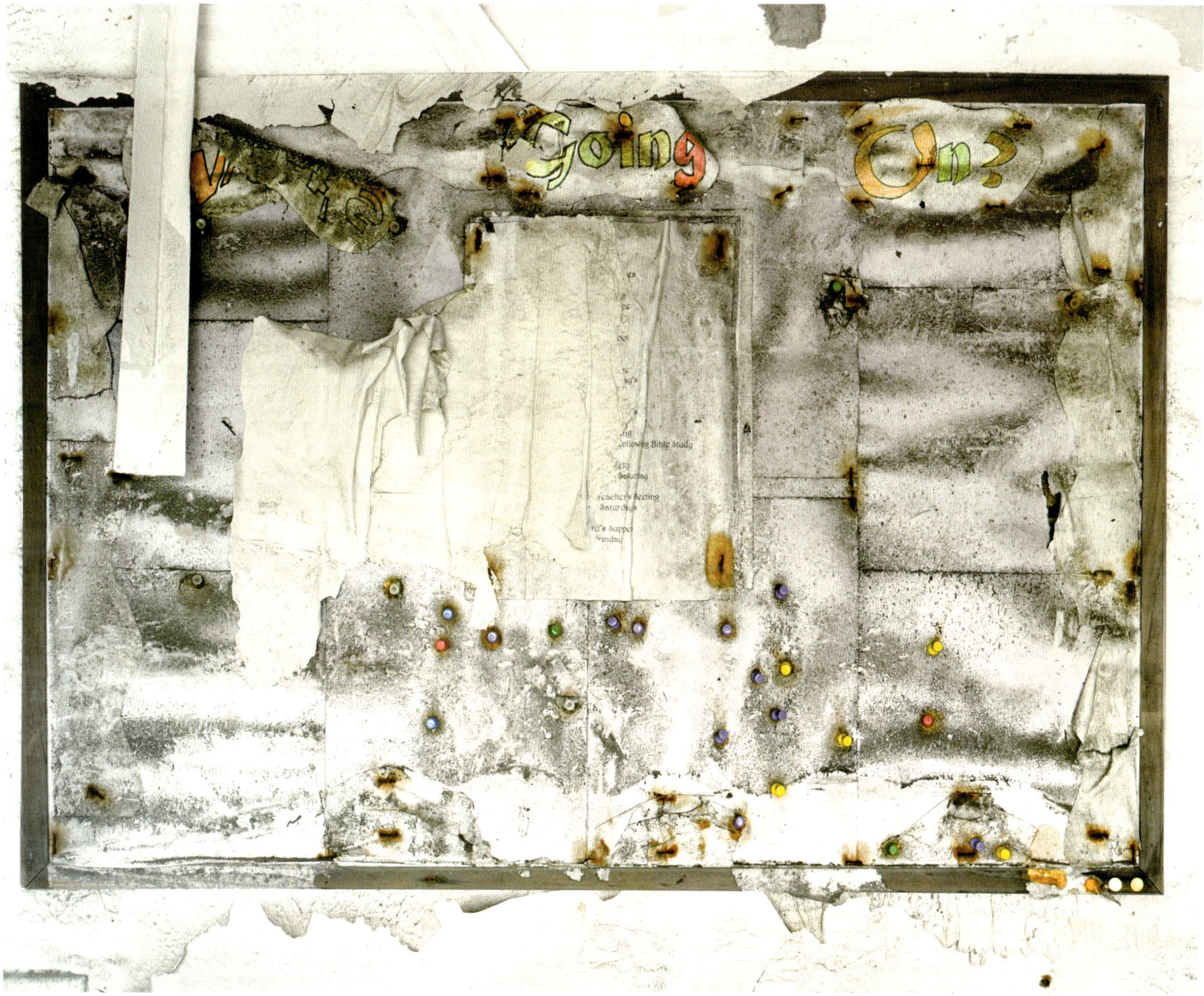
Going
On?

39. BEAUTY SPOT SALON

ST. CLAUDE AVENUE

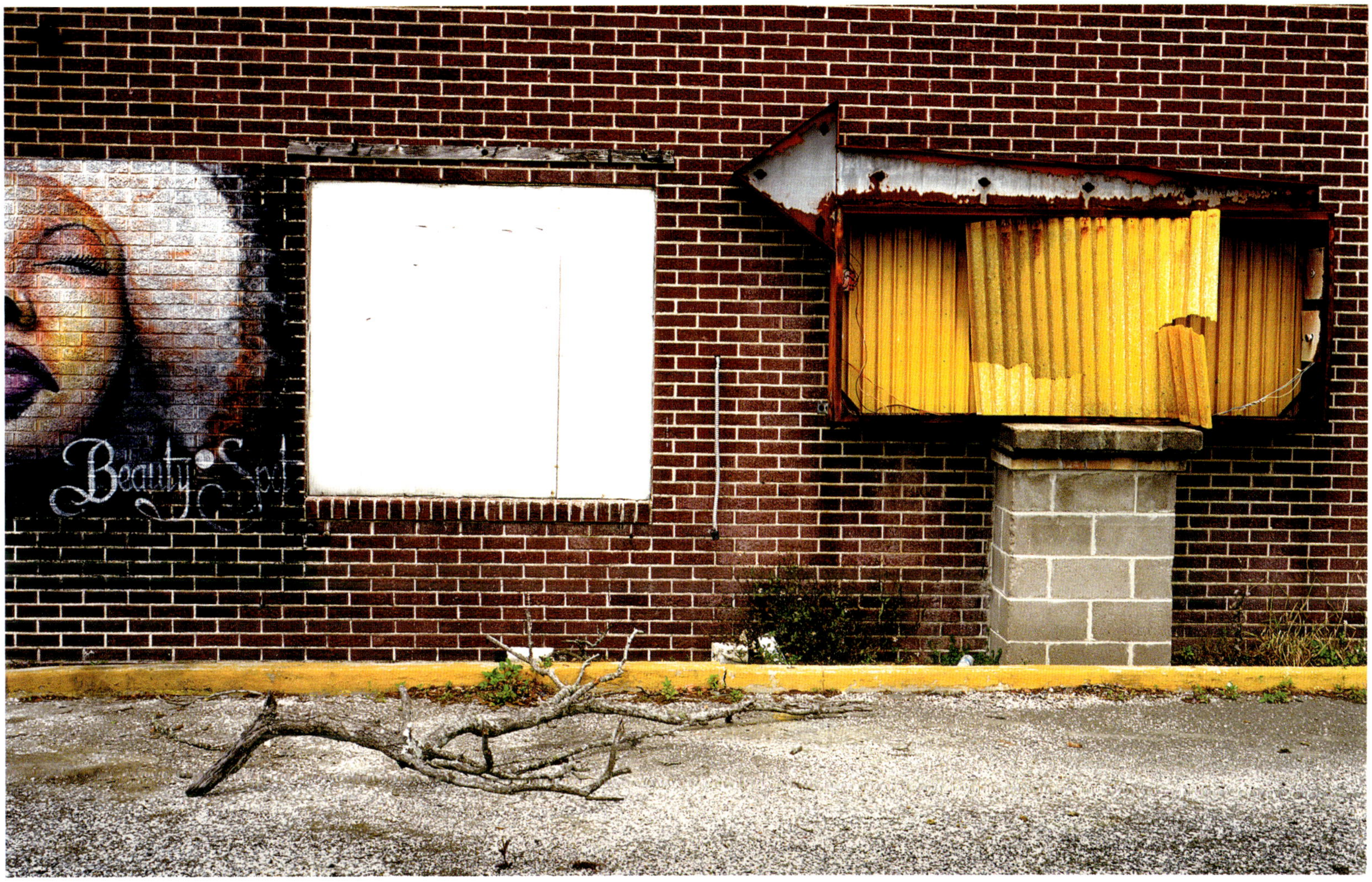
Beauty Spot

40. ANDRY STREET

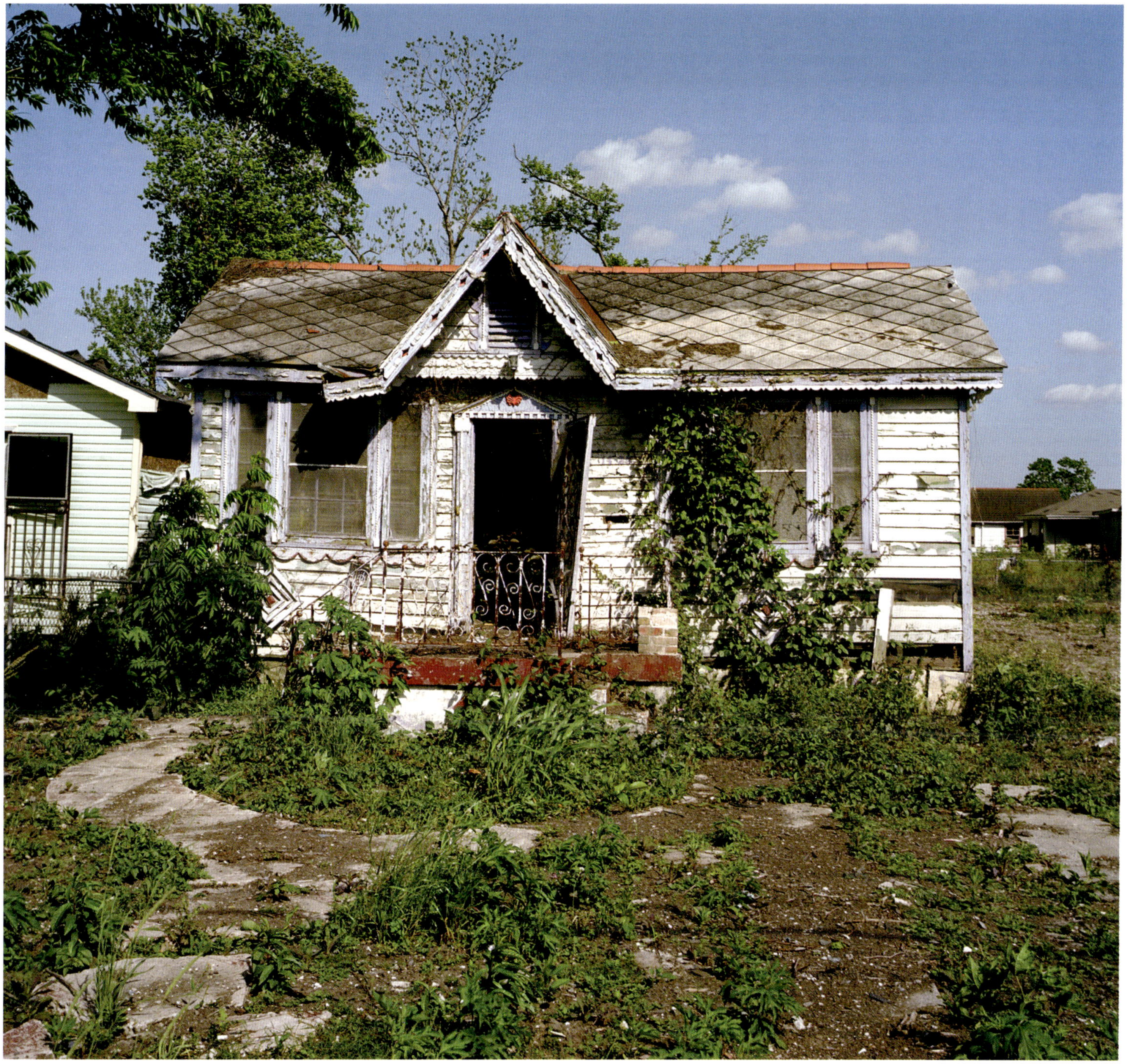

41. FORSTALL STREET

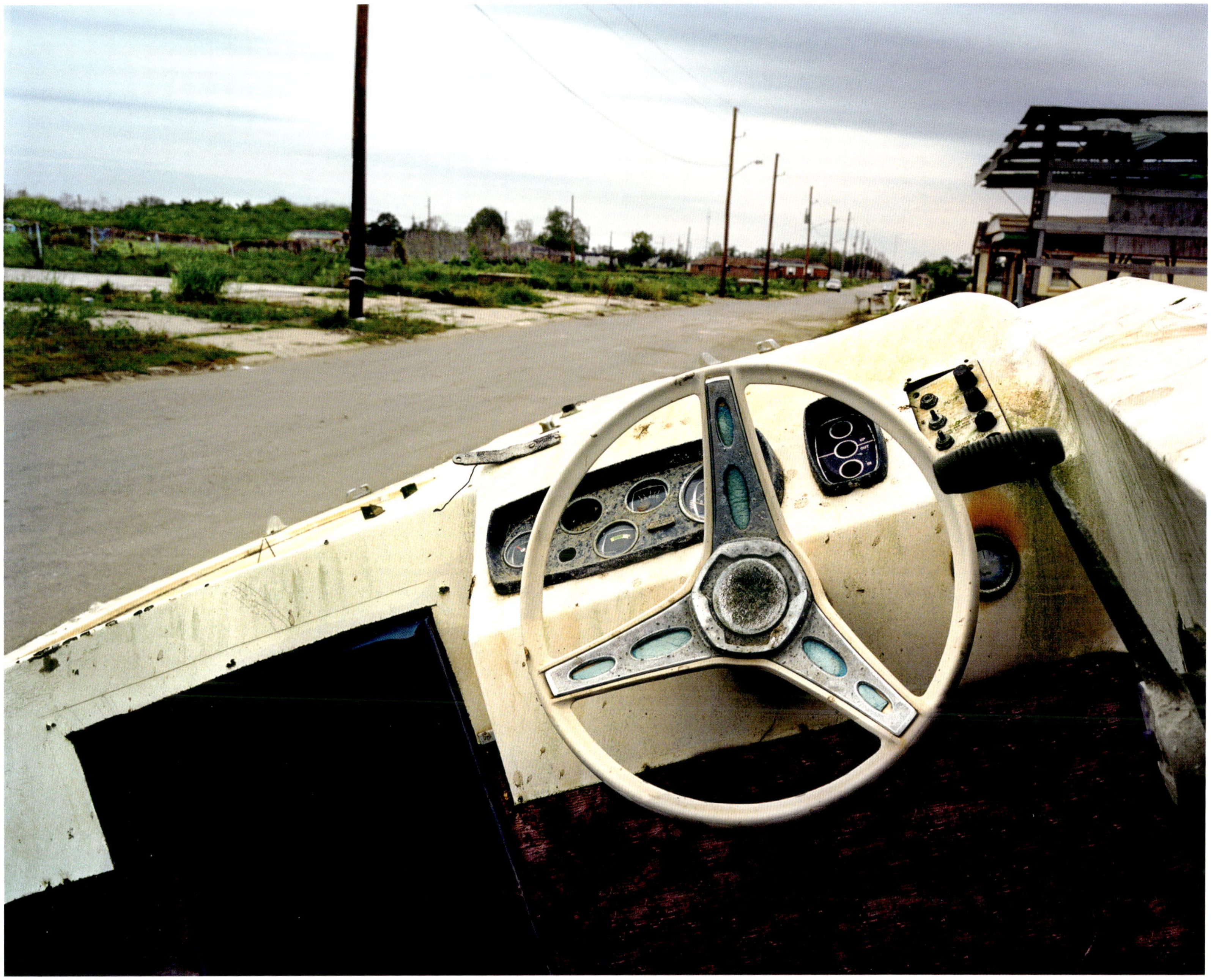

42. EMELDA EDWARDS WILLIAMS

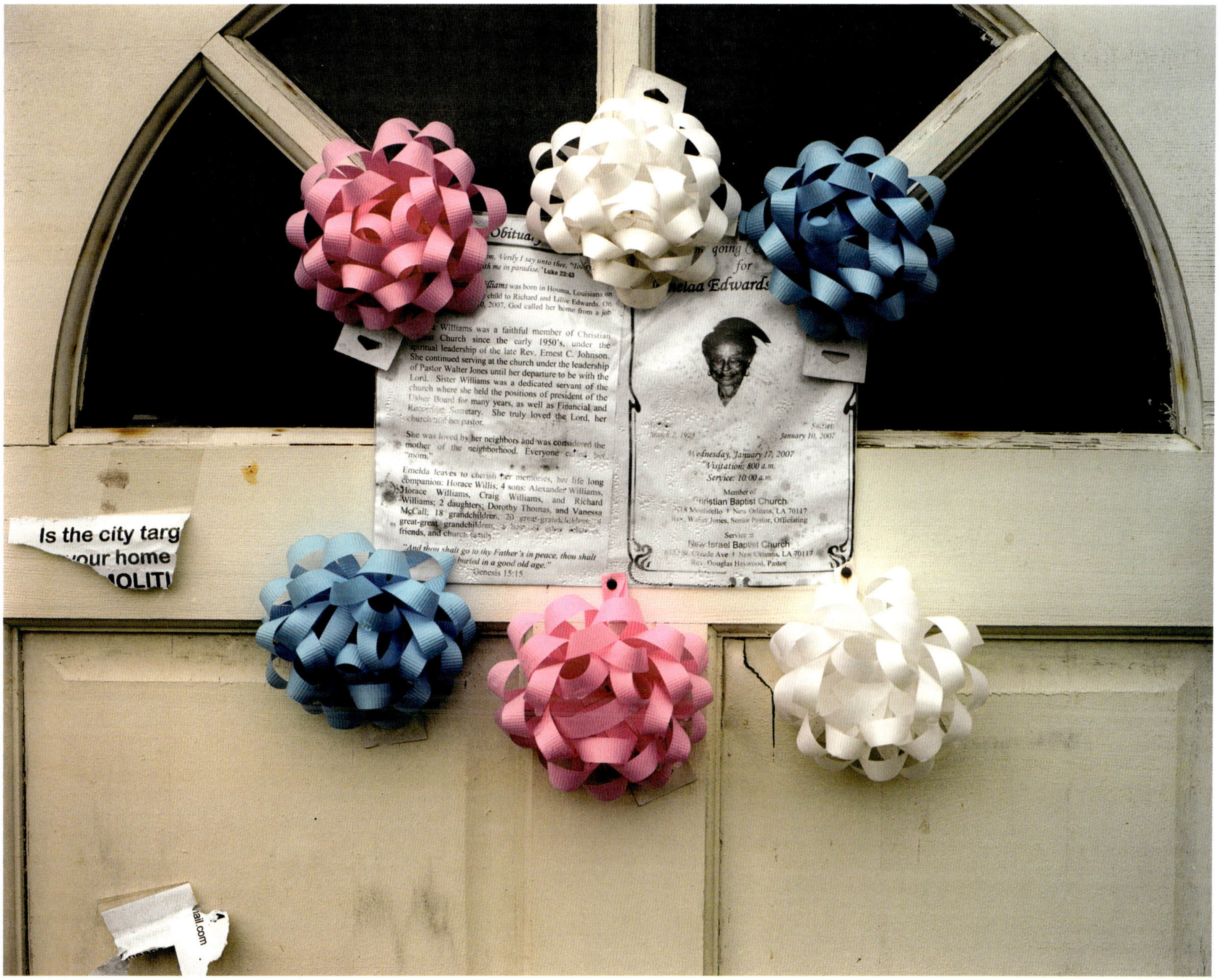

Williams was a faithful member of Christian
Church since the early 1950's, under the
spiritual leadership of the late Rev. Ernest C. Johnson.
She continued serving at the church under the leadership
of Pastor Walter Jones until her departure to be with the
Lord. Sister Williams was a dedicated servant of the
church where she held the positions of president of the
Usher Board for many years, as well as Financial and
She truly loved the Lord, her
She was loved by her neighbors and was considered the
mother of the neighborhood.
"mom."
Emelda leaves to cherish her memories, her life long
companion: Horace Willis; 4 sons: Alexander Williams,
Horace Williams, Craig Williams, and Richard
Williams; 2 daughters; Dorothy Thomas, and Vanessa
McCall; 18 grandchildren,
friends, and church
"And thou shalt go to thy Father's in peace, thou shalt
buried in a good old age."
Genesis 15:15
for
Wednesday, January 17, 2007
Visitation: 800 a.m.
Service: 10:00 a.m.
Member of
New Israel Baptist Church
Is the city targ
your home

43. LOUIS ARMSTRONG ELEMENTARY SCHOOL

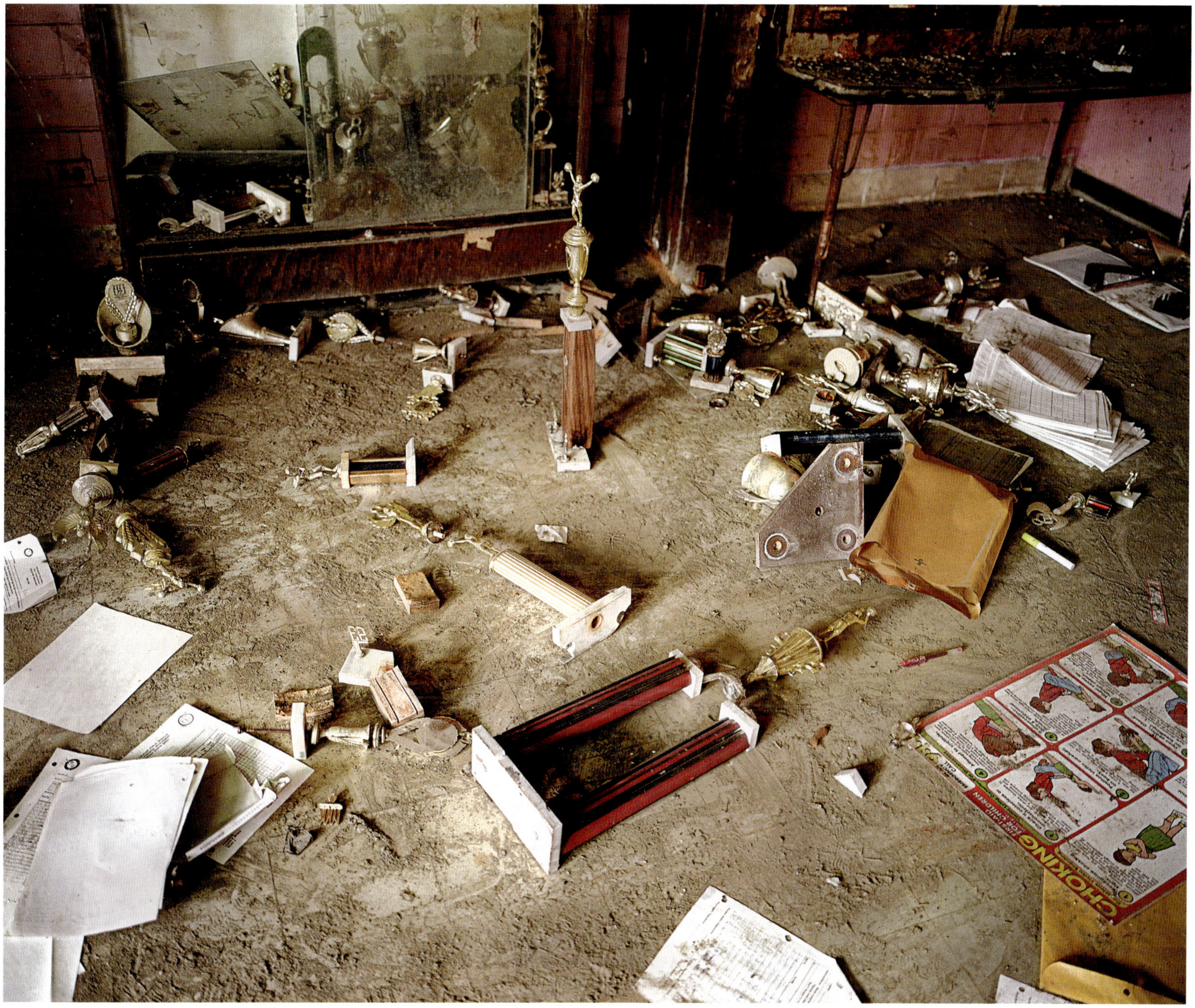
CHOKING

44. LOUIS ARMSTRONG ELEMENTARY SCHOOL

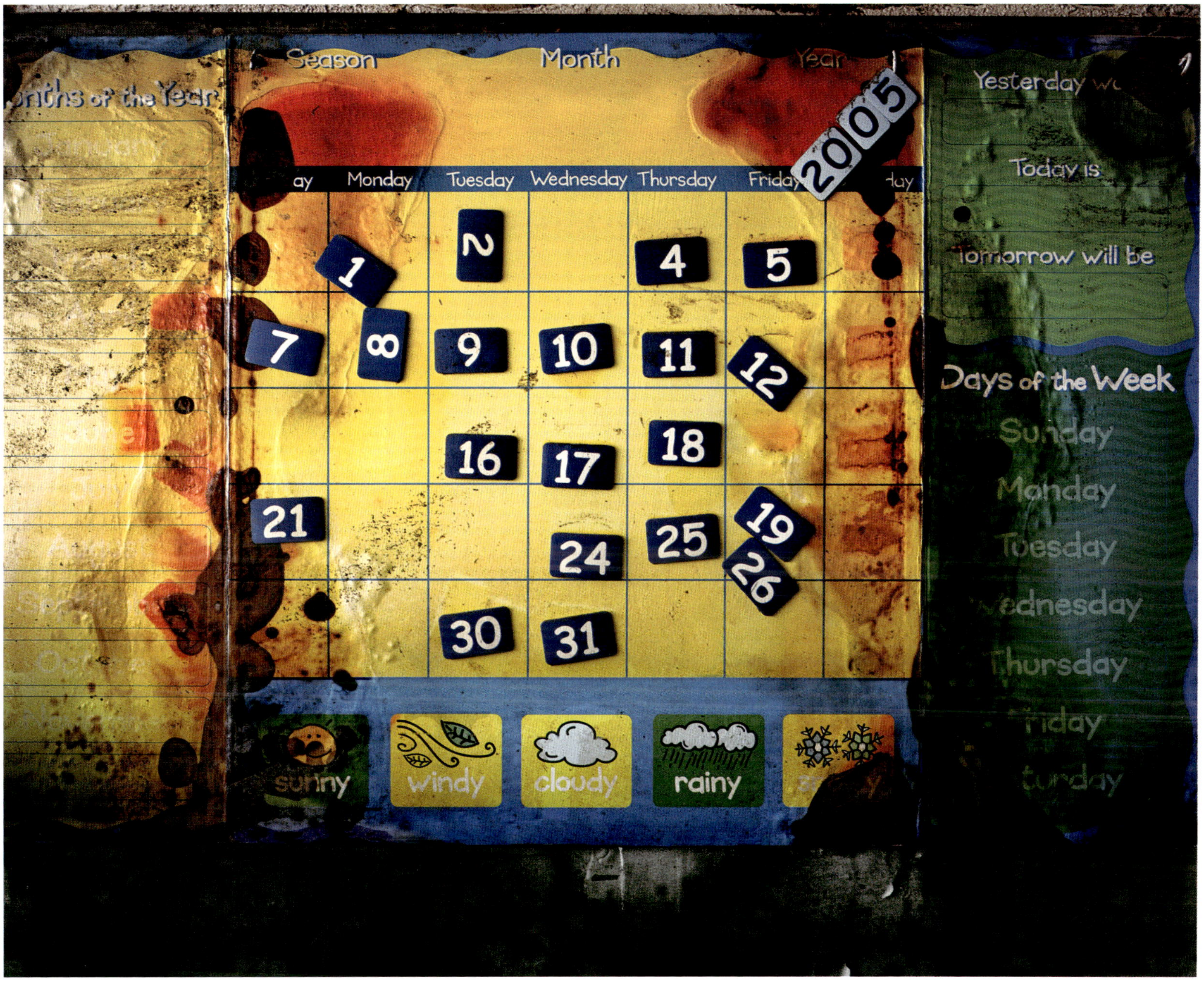
Season
Month
Year
2005
Monday
Tuesday
Wednesday
Thursday
Yesterday
Today is
Tomorrow will be
Days of the Week
Sunday
Monday
Tuesday
sunny
windy
cloudy
rainy

45. LOUIS ARMSTRONG ELEMENTARY SCHOOL

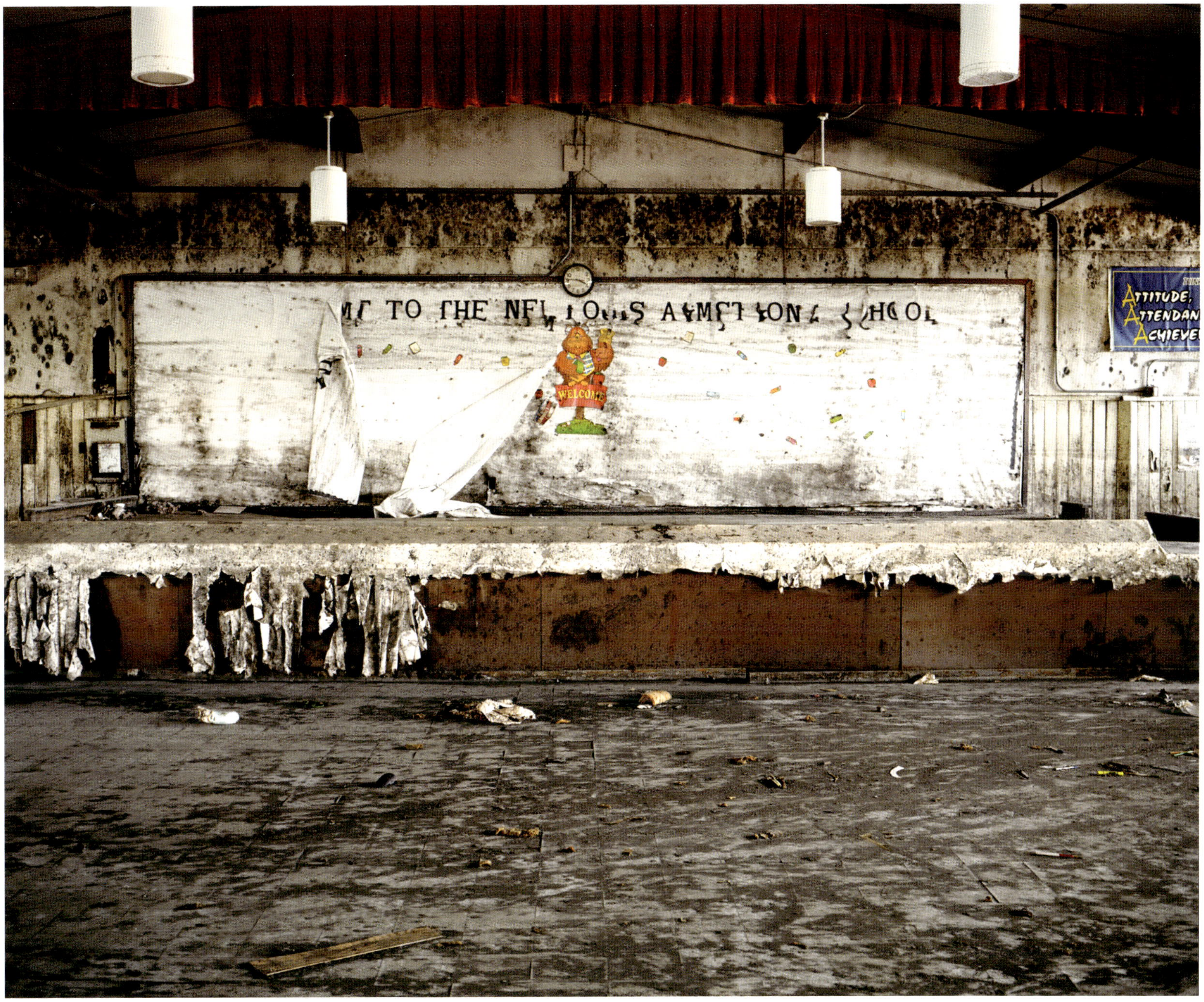
WELCOME
ATTITUDE,

46. ST. ROSE MISSIONARY BAPTIST CHURCH
FORSTALL STREET

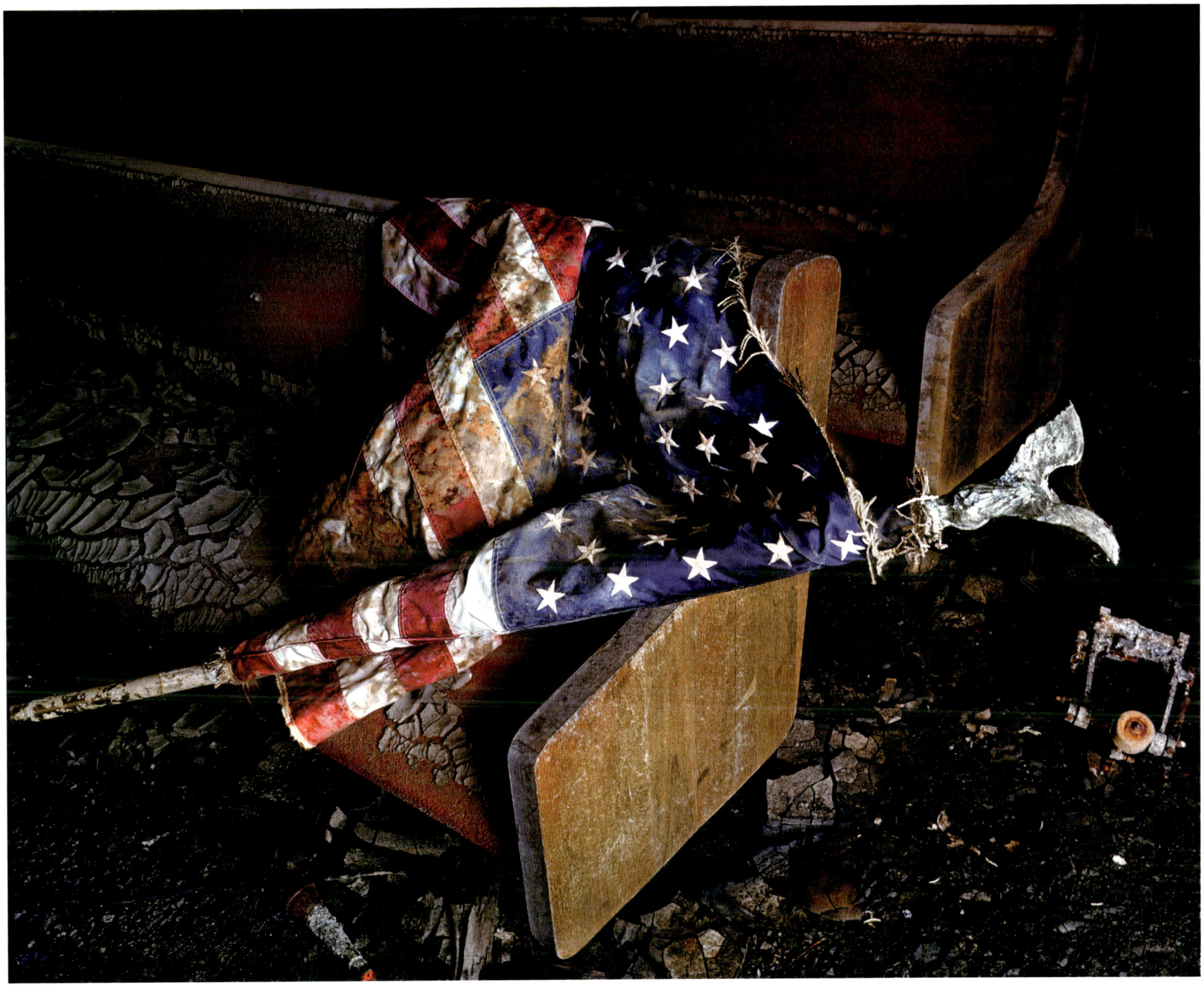

AFTERWORD

For six years, my wife led dozens of out-of-towners, including members of Congress, through parts of New Orleans that had been devastated by Hurricane Katrina and its floodwaters so they could see —and appreciate—the scope of the destruction.

She called these educational expeditions tours of devastation and hope. Although there was plenty of devastation to behold—about 80 percent of the city was under water for weeks after the levees failed—she always liked to provide some reassurance that things were, indeed, getting better. These bright spots included the new pumping stations; Musicians' Village, where the city's music makers could find affordable housing; and the restored Dr. Martin Luther King Jr. Charter School, which had taken on 11 feet of water.

I was looking for that combination of devastation and hope on a bright April morning when I drove through the Lower 9th Ward, the part of the city that everybody has fixated on in discussions of the havoc that the monster storm wrought in terms of ravaged property and ruined lives.

Nearly nine years after Katrina roared through, there is some hope in what we New Orleanians refer to as the Lower 9, although there is still plenty of devastation.

First, the hope. From the Claiborne Avenue overpass, one can see dozens of homes that have sprouted on what had been empty lots—sites where the flood's power washed away the existing residences, leaving only foundations and front steps that lead to nothing.

About 100 of the new houses are modernistic, pastel-colored dwellings designed by renowned architects under the auspices of Brad Pitt's Make It Right Foundation. These homes, which are designed to cost no more than $150,000 apiece, look nothing like conventional New Orleans shotguns and camelbacks, but they are environmentally-friendly, wind- and flood-resistant, and energy-efficient, with solar panels on the roofs.

On street after street, there are garbage cans and mailboxes—signs of progress that people in other parts of the country probably would overlook because they seem so utterly ordinary. But for me—and, I'm sure, for the urban pioneers who have returned to this part of the city—these commonplace items are reasons to rejoice because they are evidence that normal services such as mail delivery and regular garbage collection have returned to what had been, after the storm, a barren no-man's-land.

As I drove through the area, children played in yards and people mowed their lawns—normal activities, to be sure, but quite a contrast from the area's absolute emptiness shortly after the floodwater receded. I drove under trees in full, abundant leaf that formed canopies over some blocks.

But it's hardly unalloyed sweetness and light in the Lower 9. The roads are still treacherous, with bumps and dips that force drivers to stay alert, move at a snail's pace and swerve to avoid cavernous potholes. Utility poles that were knocked sideways by Katrina's gales loom over intersections. There are heaps of bulging black garbage bags on abandoned lots throughout the neighborhood.

Clumps of houses seem to be outnumbered by vast, vacant lots occupied only by high weeds. In some cases, weeds hide houses that haven't been touched since the wind and water wrecked them. At one lot, weeds conceal most of a weathered For Sale sign.

There is a strange dynamic in the Lower 9. People have built or restored houses and proceeded to go on with their lives next to buildings that haven't been touched since the storm hit. On Caffin Avenue, for instance, I saw a man calmly painting the trim on his house next to the Congregational Baptist Church, whose shredded sign and façade don't appear to have been touched for years.

The juxtaposition of occupied homes next to abandoned dwellings or vacant lots has created what has come to be called the jack-o'-lantern effect: outposts of light and plenty of darkness at night.

An almost-eerie silence pervades the neighborhood, but not everyone objects to the hush.

Corey Hayes said he likes the quiet. "It's not bad," he said. "There's no crime. I like to be isolated."

Even though he likes where he is on St. Maurice Street, Hayes said he doesn't let his children play outside at night. One reason: He and his family live in a house flanked by two abandoned dwellings, one of which, surrounded by towering weeds, seems to have been in a state of suspended animation since the storm. The other is boarded up and owned by someone who, Hayes said, mows the grass regularly.

The dilapidated house, whose walls and windows jut at crazy angles, was supposed to be demolished, Hayes said, but nothing has happened.

"They have a lot of homeowners in the Lower 9," he said, "but a lot of them didn't come back. It is what you see. We could use some company, but I don't think anybody's going to move back here."

Many of the ravaged landmarks that John Rosenthal photographed in 2007 are gone, including the Church of the Living God on Charbonnet Street, which was the subject of two pictures: one of the church itself, another of its ruined organ.

Another church on Charbonnet Street—the boarded-up Charbonnet Street Church of God in Christ—caught my eye because of the message spray-painted on the plywood boards where the door used to be: "Keep Out of God's House."

Beulah Land Baptist Church has rebuilt. Its multicolored windows are bright, and it is operating. Its sign bears this message: "If we can help somebody, then our living shall not be in vain. Come rejoice with us."

John Pope

ACKNOWLEDGMENTS

I am deeply grateful to Rebecca Currence, most generous of friends, who introduced me properly to her beloved city; to writer–filmmaker Lolis Eric Elie, whose early encouragement heartened me; and to Adolph Bynum, historic preservationist of Tremé, who opened doors that otherwise would have remained closed. A 2008 North Carolina Arts Council Fellowship Award gave me room to breathe, and I am appreciative.

Design by Jonathan Greene

with display set in three faces designed

by Eric Gill and with text set in Giovanni Mardersteig's

Dante Pro, originally (1957) a private press typeface

for the Officina Bodoni in Verona.